Rehabilitating Criminal Sexual Psychopaths

More than half the states in the US have legislation on sex offenders that distinguishes between those whose offense is incidental to other offenses ("felony" sexual offenders), and those who engage in "repetitive, habitual, or compulsive" sex offenses ("criminal sexual psychopaths"). This second category is the subject of this book. The legislation specifies that criminal sexual psychopaths must be treated, not punished. But treatment is problematic; the literature on various approaches finds uncertainty about the effectiveness of treatment. Pallone asks the difficult question of whether there is a prospective right to effective treatment, and notes the political and ethical questions involved in potentially more effective "Clockwork Orange" approaches. The ethical burden on mental health clinicians is heavy; despite the fact that the category "sexual psychopath" is essentially a legal, not a psychiatric, category, judges tend to follow professional recommendations as to categorization. Pallone emerges with some surprising but convincing conclusions. If the distinction between felony and psychopathic sexual offending is essentially empty, as the profession feels it is, it should be abandoned. All criminal sexual offenders should be punished, except those who opt for treatment and who are certified by mental health professionals as likely to benefit. And for those few so identified, society should be prepared to commit significant resources to their treatment. This speculation on the past, present, and future of criminal sexual deviation comes from a psychologist with a broad command of the literature and deep professional experience in the area. Combining a broad-ranging overview of the legal, criminological, and psychiatric literature on these questions, *Rehabilitating Criminal Sexual Psychopaths* raises important questions. Legal experts, criminologists, mental health professionals, and all those concerned with public policy will find it significant.

Nathaniel J. Pallone (1935–2004) was University Distinguished Professor of Psychology at the Center of Alcohol Studies, Rutgers University. He served as editor-in-chief of the *Journal of Offender Rehabilitation*. His published works include *Mental Disorder among Prisoners*.

Rehabilitating Criminal Sexual Psychopaths

Legislative Mandates, Clinical Quandaries

Nathaniel J. Pallone

Routledge
Taylor & Francis Group

LONDON AND NEW YORK

First published 1990 by Transaction Publishers

First published in paperback 2018
by Routledge
711 Third Avenue, New York, NY 10017

and by Routledge
2 Park Square, Milton Park, Abingdon, Oxon OX14 4RN

Routledge is an imprint of the Taylor & Francis Group, an informa business

© 2018 Taylor & Francis

The right of Nathaniel J. Pallone to be identified as author of this
work has been asserted by him in accordance with sections 77 and 78
of the Copyright, Designs and Patents Act 1988.

Library of Congress Cataloging-in-Publication Data
Pallone, Nathaniel J.
Rehabilitating criminal sexual psychopaths : legislative mandates,
clinical quandaries / Nathaniel J. Pallone
p. cm.
1. Sex offenders–Legal status, laws, etc.–United States. 2. Sex
offenders–Rehabilitation–United States. 3. Sex offenders–United
States.
I. Title
KF9750.5.P35
364.1'53–dc20

ISBN: 978-0-88738-340-3 (hbk)
ISBN: 978-1-4128-6533-3 (pbk)
ISBN: 978-1-351-31688-0 (ebk)

Typeset in Times New Roman
by Servis Filmsetting Ltd, Stockport, Cheshire

Contents

Preface

This volume had its remote origins in the very many "after hours" discussions I had with the late Dr. Alfred Vuocolo, with whom I had the privilege of serving as a member of New Jersey's Classification Review Board for Sex Offenders for many years before his untimely death. As a recognized authority on criminal sexual psychopath legislation, Dr. Vuocolo invited and stimulated my thinking about the sociolegal bases and implications of what it was we were about as we fulfilled our roles in the execution of the law.

But preparation of this manuscript began in earnest only during a year I spent as a visiting professor at the School of Public Health at Harvard, at the invitation of William R. Curran, Frances Gessner Lee Professor of legal medicine and health policy, to whom I am indebted in very many ways. The manuscript has, I hope, benefited from critical reading by a number of friends and colleagues. I am particularly grateful to Harold Demone, former dean of the School of Social Work at Rutgers and my office-mate at Harvard. Sir Gerhard Mueller of the Graduate School of Criminal Justice at Rutgers provided me with extraordinarily valuable insights into victimization studies. Robert Pandina of the Center for Alcohol Studies at Rutgers and Kirtley Thornton of the Center for Health Psychology, South Plainfield, helped me interpret data from the neurosciences. Donald Biggs of SUNY at Albany introduced me to his daughter's research on the history of sex crime legislation in New England. James Hennessy of Fordham played the role of devil's advocate that he has perfected in relation to my manuscripts over 20 years, though perhaps with greater zest because of his own interest in sex offenses.

Joanne Williams, my research assistant, has been particularly efficient, not to say also tolerant of my somewhat erratic demands. Adeline Tallau of the Rutgers Library of Science and Medicine and Phyllis Schulze of the National Council on Crime and Delinquency Library at the Newhouse Center for Law and Justice on the Newark campus of Rutgers have been incredibly effective in helping me locate obscure references. Letitia, my spouse and partner, has, as ever, been directly supportive in very many ways as well as understanding of my peculiar work habits.

Nathaniel J. Pallone

1   Both Guilty and Mentally Ill

Topography of a Twilight Zone

In the usual case, the issue of the mental health or illness of a defendant to charges of felony crime arises *if and only if* the defendant *elects* on his or her own initiative to plead *not guilty by reason of insanity*. Should the status of the defendant's mental illness rise to a level that meets the legislatively-defined criteria for an insanity defense in the relevant jurisdiction [*Note* 1], a judicial finding reflecting that plea is entered, so that the defendant is formally declared *not* guilty of the felonious act, with the customary result that he or she is confined to a public mental hospital (often, a hospital "for the criminally insane") until he or she has been declared no longer psychologically disordered, usually both by the mental health authorities responsible for treatment and by the court which declared the defendant "not guilty by reason of insanity" [*Note* 2]. The usual case, therefore, involves a neatly compartmentalized *disjunction* between mental illness (or, at the least, between mental illness serious enough to rise to the level of an insanity defense) and criminal guilt.

But, in more than half the states of the union, these neat compartments collapse under the weight of legislation governing sex offenders that implicitly creates a third, and *conjunctive*, category—that is, *both* guilty *and* mentally ill [*Note* 3].

Sexual Psychopaths as Both Guilty and Mentally Ill

In these states, the criminal codes distinguish between two categories of sex offenders: (1) those who commit sex offenses incidentally to other felony offenses (e.g., the burglar who rapes) or who are first-time sex offenders *and* (2) those who are identified as "repetitive, habitual, or compulsive" sex offenders. The relevant legislation typically refers to the former as *felony sex offenders* and the latter as *criminal sexual psychopaths* [*Note* 4].

As legal scholar Josephine Bulkley (1981, p. 92) put it in an American Bar Association review on the issue:

> Sexual psychopath statutes generally define such offenders as possessing a mental condition or defect which falls short of insanity. *Such persons*

are considered socially maladjusted or mentally disabled, but not legally insane or mentally ill so as to render them irresponsible for the criminal acts. Underlying these laws is the premise that the offender is unable to control his sexual acts because of this particular mental defect ... A typical definition of a sexual psychopath [extracted from the laws of the District of Columbia] is "a person, not insane, who by a course of repeated misconduct in sexual matters has evidenced such lack of power to control his sexual impulses as to be dangerous to other persons."

The distinction between *sexual psychopathy* and *insanity* is capital in the legal definition in several dimensions, for it creates a sort of Twilight Zone at the intersection of the law and the mental health sciences.

In the first instance, the legislation raises *a priori*—and *not* on the motion of the defendant—the issue of his or her mental health. The relevant laws customarily *require* examination of the accused by mental health clinicians responsible to the court prior to trial or prior to sentencing, while the laws governing the insanity defense render submission to such examination entirely volitional. Usually, there is no provision for *waiver* of examination, with the implication that the offender thereby voluntarily opts for what is virtually uniformly presumed to be the "harsher" penalty of sentencing as a felony sex offender.

A variety of issues related to Constitutional guarantees to privacy and against self-incrimination might seem thereby to be engaged. Nonetheless, the U.S. Supreme Court has upheld, in its *Allen v. Illinois* decision of 1986, the right of the state to require defendants to submit to such examination, ruling that legislatively-mandated (or, at minimum, legislatively-approbated) procedures for determining whether a particular offender should be classified as a "sexually dangerous person" in need of treatment were essentially *civil* rather than criminal in nature, holding therefore that plaintiff in the case "was not entitled to self-incrimination warnings prior to a court ordered psychiatric examination pursuant to the Illinois statute" (Wettstein, 1986, p. 330). Since such proceedings for determining classification as a sexual psychopath arise *only* within the context of adjudication of *criminal* charges, however, as distinguished forensic psychiatrist Paul Appelbaum (1987) has argued, one is hard pressed to understand the reasoning of the Court.

In the second and conceptually more salient instance, the legislation implicitly sorts those who commit sex offenses into *three* groups:

1. Those who are unable to control their behavior *only* in the sexual sphere and thus are "properly" classified as sexual psychopaths—that is, as *both* guilty *and* mentally ill.
2. Those who are unable to control their behavior in *any* sphere and thus meet the relevant legal criteria for insanity, with the result that they are exculpated from any penalty for criminal behavior—that is, those who are adjudicated as *mentally ill but not guilty* [*Note 5*].

3. Those who are neither so mentally disordered as to be classified as legally insane nor as sexually psychopathic but are "merely" guilty of felony crimes which are sexual in nature and thus are adjudicated as *guilty but not mentally ill.*

Differential Penalties

For those adjudicated as "felony sex offenders," the criminal codes prescribe typical felony-style sentences, to be served in prison facilities operated by state *correctional* authorities, and, in the main, through minimum-maximum sentencing procedures (e.g., *between 12 and 15 years*, etc.). Along with other felony offenders, these offenders become eligible for parole only after serving a portion of their terms (usually, between 25% and 33% of their minimum sentences), and the criteria under which the parole decision is made are the same as apply to all punitively incarcerated inmates (e.g., "institutional adjustment"). When judicial discretion is exercised in such a way that a custodial sentence is suspended and the convicted offender is instead placed on probation, there is no particular presumption that he or she should participate in mental health treatment as a condition of such probation.

For the "criminal sexual psychopath," however, the legislation usually prescribes confinement for mental health "treatment" in a specialized facility, operated in some states by the *correctional* authority but in other states by the *mental health* authority. Sentences are typically keyed only to maxima (*e.g., not to exceed 15 years*), but, peculiarly in light of what appears to be the common thread in legislative intent, in some states with judicial discretion to stipulate a "mandatory minimum."

Differential Pathways to Release

Release from such "confinement for treatment" tends to follow legislatively and judicially established pathways for release from those institutions which are governed by the responsible authority (i.e., *either* the state's psychiatric hospital authority, typically responsible to a division or department of health, *or* the correctional authority). When judicial discretion is exercised in these cases in such a way that a custodial sentence is suspended and the convicted offender instead placed on probation, it is customary that he or she is required to participate in mental health treatment as a condition of probation and, as a condition of release from probation, to present evidence of significant therapeutic change.

In the case of the criminal sexual psychopath confined under jurisdiction of the *mental health authority*, release from confinement will follow the pathways legislatively and judicially established to govern release from *criminal* commitments for psychiatric hospitalization. In states in which the treatment facility is controlled by the *correctional authority*, release will follow the pathway established for the granting of parole, typically with some unusual inflections. In such cases, parole is customarily granted only upon satisfaction of *clinical* criteria that the offender is "cured" or "no longer presents a danger to society," and the parole process may be a three-stage affair, involving review by institutional staff, by a panel of extra-institutional mental health experts who constitute a clinical "dangerousness review" or "pre-parole" board, and by the state parole authority. For these offenders, there is *no presumptive right to parole*, with all the Fourteenth Amendment guarantees associated therewith. Similarly, release from probation for those offenders for whom mental health treatment has been imposed as a condition will pivot upon demonstration that such treatment has been so effective as to yield "cure" or to render the offender no longer a threat to society.

Clinically Esoteric Inclusionary Criteria

Inclusionary criteria, particularly as applied to offenders who are categorized as "compulsive" rather than as habitual or repetitive (that is, those for whom such categorization is predicated on mental health assessment rather than on a review of prior criminal record alone), often tend to be clinically esoteric, indeed perhaps sufficiently so as to give rise to questions about "due process."

Yet, while the relevant legislation has been repeatedly questioned in various jurisdictions, from *Miller v. Overholser* in 1953 onward, a variety of judicial decisions have *constrained but maintained* the rectitude of legislatively-prescribed and judicially-imposed mental health treatment for *one* class of sex offender.

Notes

1. The *M'Naghten Rule* has long been precedental in determining criminal culpability in nations which follow British common law. Promulgated in the decision of an English court in 1843 (and doubtless influenced by the views of Joseph Pritchard, an English physician who had earlier invented a mental illness he termed "moral insanity" to explain criminal behavior), in a case in which the secretary to a cabinet officer was murdered by a disappointed office seeker who declared that he had been commanded by God to kill the Prime Minister, the M'Naghten Rule holds that legal culpability attaches to an otherwise criminal act only when the behaver knows in advance that the contemplated behavior counters moral principle and/or positive law *and* when he or she is *free to choose* to behave or not to behave. As the editors of an important monograph commissioned by the Royal College of Psychiatrists (West & Walk, 1977, p.1) put it: "If an offender knew that what he was doing was wrong, he was legally sane and subject to punishment." Thus, under M'Naghten, a person who is incapable of distinguishing "wrong" from "right" is *not* to be held legally culpable. On this side of the Atlantic, two cases in the last quarter of the last century (*Parsons v. the State of Alabama*, adjudicated in 1887, and *Davis v. United States*, adjudicated a decade later) added the "irresistible impulse" test, which exculpates a person who is incapable of resisting an impulse propelling him or her to a wrong or legally criminal act (Stone, 1976, p. 229). In 1954, the U.S. District Court for the District of Columbia specifically included prior mental illness in the catalog of acceptable justifications for a claim of nonculpability under M'Naghten

by holding that "an accused is not criminally responsible if his unlawful act was the product of mental disease." Following the name of the defendant (Durham) and the presiding justice (Bazelon) in the case, the resultant principle is called the *Durham Test* or the *Bazelon Rule.*

Over the course of nearly a century and a half, a variety of other justifications have been accepted by the courts under M'Naghten to explain either the incapacity to distinguish right from wrong or the incapacity to resist the impulse to behave criminally, including intellectual deficiency and even habitual criminal behavior itself (Rogers, 1986, pp. 39–90). Hence, in its model penal code, the American Law Institute proposed a more comprehensive statement such that "A person is not responsible for criminal conduct if, at the time of such conduct, as a result of mental disease or defect he lacks substantial capacity either to appreciate the criminality of his conduct or to conform his conduct to the requirement of law. [But] the terms 'mental disease or defect' do not include an abnormality manifested only by repeated criminal or otherwise antisocial conduct" (Stone, 1976, p. 230). That formulation, or a close variant, has by now been legislatively adopted in most states, both as the legal definition of insanity and as part of a catalog of "mitigating factors," the presence of which may not exculpate an alleged offender but influences the severity of the sanction imposed upon conviction. Other mitigating factors may include such variables as the influence of mood-altering drugs or alcohol, the prior relationship between the victim and the alleged offender, whether the victim in some way invited or colluded in his or her own victimization, etc. A litany of mitigating factors may be offset by "aggravating factors," such as the degree of demonstrable premeditation, whether the allegedly criminal act was performed during the commission of another criminal act, etc. Predictably, expert witnesses for the defense tend to find evidence of insanity or of mitigating factors, while expert witnesses for the prosecution typically fail to find such evidence, so that closely contested trials sometimes resemble three-ring circuses abounding with conflicting testimony. Such was the case in the trial of John Hinckley after his attempt to assassinate Ronald Reagan, and the press coverage of this aspect of the Hinckley trial served to underscore emphatically deep divisions in the mental health community (Stone, 1984). Virtually as a direct result of the Hinckley trial, or at least of the press reports thereof, the American Psychiatric Association (1984) issued a statement on the insanity defense that in essence endorsed the American Law Institute definition but added the important contingencies that "the terms mental disease or mental retardation include only those severely abnormal mental conditions that grossly and demonstrably impair a person's perception or understanding of reality and that are not attributable primarily to the voluntary ingestion of alcohol or other psychoactive substances."

Whatever the terms of the conceptual debate, it is the M'Naghten Rule and the Durham Test or their close variants that are reflected in positive law, and these defenses may be invoked only in cases in which an accused pleads "not guilty by reason of insanity" in accordance with the legal definition of insanity promulgated in specific jurisdictions (i.e., the several states and the Federal court system). Like criminality, however, *insanity* is fundamentally a legal rather than a psychological or psychiatric construct; its meaning, even in the world of criminal law and adjudication, is essentially vague but generally held to imply the incapacity to distinguish right from wrong, whether under terms of positive law or those of a pristine moral code.

The closest analogue one finds to *insanity* as a legal construct in the lexicon of psychology and psychiatry is the term *psychopathic deviation*, included in the first edition (1952) of the American Psychiatric Association's *Diagnostic and Statistical Manual of Mental Disorders* as a mental illness clearly reminiscent of Pritchard's formulation, but excluded from the roster of mental illnesses in the second (1968), third (1980), and "third-revised" (1987) editions. But the analogue largely begged the question by providing essentially only a circular definition, in which insanity was defined by psychopathic deviation and psychopathic deviation by insanity. The Third Edition's successor term, *anti-social personality disorder*, appropriately avoids notions like the incapacity to form moral judgments in favor of a focus on *patterns of socially responsible and irresponsible behavior*. Yet the only readily discernible empirical referent in these varying terms is likely a *generalized tendency to underestimate the costs and risks*, both for the behaver and for others affected by his or her behavior, *attached to behaving in formally proscribed ways*, implying an element of *reckless disregard for the consequences of behavior*, for which the term "psychopathic deviation" may be as descriptive as any other.

2. Contextually, Phillips, Worlf & Coons (1988) reported that a *successful* plea of insanity occurred in less than one percent of *all* criminal cases in the state of Alaska over a four year period; whether that figure varies state by state is not known. But, in the United Kingdom, Chiswick (1987) observed that the incidence of a judicial determination of insanity in criminal trials was ten times greater in Scotland than in England and Wales. One might expect, then, considerable variation between the several states of the Union.

There is a substantial body of literature, both in legal and in mental health studies, concerning a "successful" insanity plea and its after-math. In some jurisdictions, release from a criminal commitment for inpatient treatment following a successful insanity plea requires only the decision of the superintendent of the treating hospital; in others, release requires the decision of a criminal court judge based on the recommendation of the hospital superintendent, itself presumably contingent upon that of the mental health clinicians principally responsible for the delivery of treatment; in yet others, release requires the decision of a jury analogous to that which delivered the "not guilty by reason of insanity" verdict in the first place. Under color of the Fourteenth Amendment's guarantee against the restriction of liberty without due process, the person incarcerated in a mental institution as the result of criminal commitment has the right to challenge any and all of these recommendations and decisions at court. Indeed, Miller, Maier, Blancke & Doren (1986) have interpreted litigiousness on the part of criminally committed mental patients as a form of resistance to treatment.

Studies focussing on the length of time spent in inpatient treatment as a consequence of criminal commitment typically indicate a minimum of five years, with nearly nine as the effective maximum; these figures contrast sharply with the number of *weeks* customarily spent in inpatient treatment in voluntary or civil commitments.

Shapiro (1984, pp. 28–50) provides a succinct history of the development of the construct of criminal responsibility. For the historically minded, Pankratz (1984) has offered a perspective on nineteenth century views on criminal insanity in the U.S. through a content analysis of the *American Journal of Insanity*, the official publication of the "alienists" who studied such phenomena from the 1860s to 1880s. Other conceptual and operational issues are reviewed by Beckham, Annis & Gustafson (1989); Boehnert (1985); Faulstich (1984); Finkel & Handel (1989); Howard & Clark (1985); Luckey & Berman (1981); Mitchell (1986); Rachlin, Halpern & Portnow (1984); Rogers, Cavanaugh, Seman & Harris (1984); Rogers & Zimbarg (1987); and Smith, (1980).

3. Since 1975, the laws of Michigan have permitted a finding of "guilty but mentally ill" in respect of *any* criminal charge. The relevant legislation hinges upon evidence of "a substantial disorder of thought or mood which significantly impairs judgment, behavior, capacity to recognize reality, or ability to cope with the ordinary

demands of life." For a review of conceptual, legal, and practical issues engendered in the application of the "guilty but mentally ill" standard in Michigan and in other states in which it or a close analogue has been adopted, see Rogers (1986, pp. 16–18, 55–59).

4. Vuocolo (1968) reported the number of states with active criminal sexual psychopath legislation as 35. A more recent survey by Brunette & Sales (1980) puts the number at 27: Alabama, California, Colorado, Connecticut, the District of Columbia, Florida, Georgia, Illinois, Indiana, Maryland, Massachusetts, Minnesota, Mississippi, Missouri, Nebraska, Nevada, New Hampshire, New Jersey, Ohio, Oregon, Pennsylvania, Tennessee, Utah, Virginia, Washington, Wisconsin, Wyoming. Because criminal codes undergo frequent revision, whether wholesale or piecemeal, and in view of legal challenges to one or another aspect of criminal sexual psychopath legislation in cases brought on behalf of convicted offenders who have (and in some cases, have not, but who would have preferred to have) been sentenced under the terms of such legislation, the number of states with such legislation is likely to vary annually. The legislation is relatively silent, however, on the burglar who burgles *because* he is seeking a prospective victim for rape or sexual assault (Duffy & Hirshberg, 1965; Revitch, 1983; Slovenko, 1965).

5. Case law interpreting, broadening, or constraining criminal code formulations on the insanity plea grows apace. Thus, a Federal circuit court (U.S. *v. Gould*, 741 F.2D, 45, 1984) has rejected a history of "pathological gambling" in support of a plea of insanity, but the supreme courts of two states (*Connecticut v. Lafferty*, 472 A.2D 1275, 1984; *New York v. Escobar*, 462 NE.2D 1171, 1984) have interpreted the laws of their respective states as permitting the confinement of property offenders who are acquitted after successfully pleading not guilty by reason of insanity in consequence of putative "dangerousness to property" even when violent behavior (in the usual sense of "imminent dangerousness to self or others") is not predictable.

Perhaps in response to such changes in judicial interpretation, contemporary research on the antecedents and sequelae to an insanity plea has burgeoned in the recent past. In a study of factors associated with a successful insanity plea in one county in New York during a ten-year period, Steadman, Keitner, Braff & Arvanites (1983) reported that 83% of all such pleas were successful; but they discerned no significant relationships between acquittal and demographic factors, criminal history, severity of the current alleged offense, or history of psychiatric hospitalization. An investigation by Rogers, Cavanaugh, Seman & Harris (1984) reports convergence between clinical opinion and judicial determination in 89% of the 112 cases they studied; curiously, convergence was observed at 100% in the case of female defendants. In an inventive study of the degree of congruence between the M'Naghten and the American Law Institute standards for the insanity defense, Silver & Spodak (1983) retrospectively analyzed cases seen in one forensic psychiatric hospital, finding convergent conclusions in 95% of the cases.

In an intriguing *follow-up* study of all persons found not guilty by reason of insanity in New York state between 1971 and 1976 and subsequently placed in state psychiatric institutions, Pasewark, Pantile & Steadman (1979) reported that, in comparison to other admittees, the "criminally insane" group tended to be proportionately more white and older, without a history of previous psychiatric hospitalizations, and with minimal or no prior records of criminal activity. They cited a discharge rate on the order of 35% over a five-year period, with the period of hospitalization ranging from one to 1235 days. Those data contrast markedly with the findings of Kahn & Raifman (1981) in a 23-year follow-up study of accused offenders who invoked an insanity plea, with no significant difference observed in period of confinement between the third of the sample who pled successfully and were remanded to a state psychiatric hospital and the two-thirds whose pleas were rejected, were found guilty, and imprisoned. Similarly, in New Zealand, Medlicott (1976) reported in a follow-up over a period of 35 years that subjects found "not guilty on psychiatric grounds were likely to be held for longer periods than those [adjudicated] as criminals."

With respect to criminal recidivism, in a five-year follow-up study of subjects released from mental hospitals in Maryland in comparison to a group of offenders who had been released on parole (and whose mental status at the time of the offense had presumably not been at issue), Cohen, Spodak, Silver & Williams (1988) found a higher rate of re-arrest among paroled offenders (65%) than among insanity acquitees (54%). In contrast, Lamb, Weinberger & Gross (1988) reported that 32% of their sample of defendants found not guilty by reason of insanity who had subsequently been placed in judicially-mandated *outpatient* treatment rather than confined in psychiatric hospitals were re-arrested during a five-year follow-up period, three quarters of the time for crimes of violence; in addition, 47% of these subjects had subsequently been placed in psychiatric hospitals. In rather sharp contrast, however, only 2% of the insanity acquitees who had been placed in court-ordered outpatient treatment studied by Cavanaugh & Wasyliw (1985) recidivated criminally during a two-year follow-up period.

Perhaps because passage of the Federal Community Mental Health Act of 1963 produced a pervasive movement in the U.S.toward the de-institutionalization of state psychiatric hospital patients however committed (Pallone, 1986, pp. 32–36; Torrey, 1988), Fein (1984) has contended that "the insanity acquittal may retard the treatment of mentally disordered and violent offenders [because] failure to assign responsibility to a mentally disordered offender may lessen his or her initiative and emotional opportunity to make needed changes in perceptions and functioning." He thus seems to argue in favor of the British system whereby an accused offender may be found "guilty, but with diminished responsibility," and subsequently, virtually at judicial discretion, be confined for treatment in a psychiatric hospital *or* incarcerated in a correctional facility (Beigel, 1983; Dell, 1983; Dell & Smith, 1983). Congruently, Bush (1983) has observed that, even when the insanity plea is not successful (as in 17% of the Steadman et al. sample), it is likely that some discernible psychopathological condition underlay the criminal behavior; in such instances, he recommends "treatment for the guilty" in prison settings. However, Halleck (1987), a distinguished forensic psychiatrist, believes that "the guilty but mentally ill alternative offers no new advantages to offenders and can hardly be distinguished from an ordinary criminal conviction, unless it is accompanied by a firm commitment on the part of the state to expand its treatment resources and provide offenders with effective treatment. So far, no evidence shows that this is happening."

By the mid-1980s, a standardized method for assessing whether the circumstances of an alleged offense and background factors associated with the accused offender met the M'Naghten standard, the American Law Institute standard, or the "guilty but mentally ill" standard had been developed and commercially marketed (Rogers, Seman & Wasyliw, 1983); a second method designed to function as a gross screen for "false positives" against the M'Naghten standard was under development (Slobogin, Melton & Showalter, 1984); and an instrument for the rapid assessment of competency to stand trial, in its turn largely dependent on the capacity to participate meaningfully in the preparation of a defense, was similarly under development (Nicholson, 1988).

2 The Legislative Basis

Genesis of a Twilight Zone

In his *Insanity: The Idea and Its Consequences*, maverick psychiatrist Thomas Szasz (1987, pp. 79–80) acerbically lampoons what he calls the politics of inventing and discarding psychiatric diagnostic categories, or "making and unmaking mental illness":

> the way psychiatric diagnoses are now made ... differs from the way they were made a hundred years ago ... The change in the technique for generating new psychiatric categories is not technological, but political. A century ago ... new psychiatric discoveries were made by *individuals* ... No individual American today would dare to do such a thing; it would be unseemly to be so individualistic, so autocratic, so undemocratic. Ours is the age of psychiatric "group think" ... The APA [American Psychiatric Association] now has *task forces* and *consensus groups* to make and unmake psychiatric diagnostic categories ... Now we have psychiatric democracy or mobocracy, that is, psychopathology by consensus.

The "creation" of sexual psychopathy as a "diagnostic" category with massive legal and criminal justice ramifications seems to constitute a particular instance of creation of a kind of psychopathology by *legislative "group think"* that, indeed, even runs counter to contemporary psychiatric group think.

Nor should one reasonably expect otherwise. The range of sexual behaviors proscribed by law constitutes a vast array, from forcible rape in all jurisdictions to consenting unions between adults of the same sex in some jurisdictions, from public exhibition of one's genitals to mutually agreeable unions in private between partners on either side of the "age of consent." However much legislators may be persuaded that a single category labeled "sexual psychopathy" constitutes a defensible catch-all, few members of the mental health community would ascribe similar engines for behavior to the 19-year-old who sexually unites with a willing 15-year-old of the opposite sex *and* to the 19-year-old who forces himself upon a 65-year-old victim at knife point *or* to the 19-year-old who willingly unites with another 19-year-old of his or her own sex.

Legislative Control of Sexual Behavior

In its *Psychiatry and Sex Psychopath Legislation: The '30s to the '80s* (1977, pp. 847–852), the Group for the Advancement of Psychiatry traces the legislative control of sexual behavior in nations that follow the tradition of British common law to the Statutes of Westminster enacted in 1275, when the jurisdiction of the Crown was extended "to cover the forcible rape of ... women ... and the principle of statutory rape for minors was established." The legislation initially imposed a penalty of but two years' imprisonment, but by 1285 "the statute was amended to make rape a felony punishable by death."

In the New World, the Body of Liberties enacted by the Massachusetts Bay Colony in 1648 similarly defined rape (as well as anal intercourse "with man or beast" and adultery "with a married or espoused woman") as a capital offense [Note 1]. Other colonies, and later states, followed the British tradition reflected in that early Massachusetts legislation in respect of the sanction for rape until the very recent past, when the U.S. Supreme Court determined, in the *Coker v. Georgia* decision of 1977, that death constitutes a "grossly disproportionate and excessive penalty when imposed for the rape of an adult woman" that does not end in homicide [Note 2].

The British tradition also formally proscribed a variety of other sexual behaviors, even among consenting adults, with a variety of sanctions ranging from imprisonment to public humiliation (a scarlet *A* to be worn for a lifetime in the case of adultery, a scarlet *I* in the case of incest). While incest and pedophilia almost universally remain criminal offenses with severe penalties, the sanctions for adultery, fornication, and other sexual behaviors between consenting adults have been modified over the course of the years both in England and the United States, but often in what is appropriately described as a

> haphazard manner ... that had little connection either with the harmfulness or prevalence of a particular offense ... For example, in England intercourse *per anum* by a man with his wife (buggery) is still subject to life imprisonment while the same act between two males in private is not a crime (Group for the Advancement of Psychiatry, 1977, p. 847).

Criminal prosecution of proscribed sexual behavior between consenting adults, whether homosexual or heterosexual, is quite another matter. Perhaps the most concise statement that can be made is that, by the time the American Psychiatric Association formally expelled homosexuality from its diagnostic lexicon in the mid-1970s, law enforcement authorities in most jurisdictions had long since abandoned efforts at apprehension and prosecution.

In urging reform of antiquated legislation governing sexual behavior (implicitly, between consenting adults) when such legislation no longer reflects contemporary community standards, the Group for the Advancement of Psychiatry (1950, p. 2), in a report published contemporaneously with the first Kinsey Reports on the sexual behavior of American adults and prepared by a committee to which Dr. Kinsey had been a consultant, had opined that

> 6 million homosexual acts take place each year for every 20 convictions.
>   And similarly, at a time when adultery constituted criminal behavior in most U.S. jurisdictions:
>   In the area of extramarital copulation, the frequency-to-conviction ratio is nearly 30 to 40 million to 300.

A decade and a half later, at a time when the American Law Institute affiliated with the American Bar Association was in the process of constructing a model penal code for the states, Yale law professor Fred Rodell (1965) urged "change or repeal of our outmoded sex crime laws which are regularly broken or ignored," while simultaneously disavowing advocacy of "a loosening of morals."

Sexual Psychopath Legislation in the United States

A succinct history of what he calls "special sex legislation" not only in the various states of the Union but throughout the "first world" is provided by the late Alfred Vuocolo (1968) in his landmark volume *The Repetitive Sex Offender* [*Note* 3]. Vuocolo's work is instructive in the first instance for its comparative historical analyses of legislation governing sex crimes. At the time of publication, for example, Norway and Sweden punished rape with a maximum penalty of 10 years rather than the 30-year penalties that prevailed in many jurisdictions in the various U.S. states, with the death penalty common for cross-race rapes in the American South; Denmark legislatively provided for voluntary castration in 1929 and in 1935 introduced compulsory castration; England, France, Switzerland, and Germany provided legislatively for what amounts to life imprisonment through "preventive detention" for repetitive offenders.

Vuocolo traces sexual psychopath legislation in the United States to the Defective Delinquent Laws enacted in Massachusetts in 1911, followed by essentially similar legislation in Pennsylvania in 1933. But the first legislation which specifically addressed the "habitual sex offender" was enacted by Michigan in 1937. In that legislation, "an individual who was convicted or pled guilty to a sex crime and was considered *not insane but a sex pervert*, and appeared to be suffering from a mental disorder with sex deviation and with repetitive and dangerous elements ... could be committed to the state hospital for an indeterminate period" (Vuocolo, 1968, p. 25).

A year later, Illinois adopted similar legislation, and California, Ohio, and Minnesota enacted such legislation in 1939; these states were followed by Massachusetts and Washington in 1947; the District of Columbia in

1948; Nebraska, New Jersey, New York, and New Hampshire in 1949; and, after publication in 1950 of an influential position paper on psychiatrically deviant sex offenders by the Committee on Forensic Psychiatry (whose members included such luminaries as Walter Bromberg, Hervey Cleckley, and Manfred Guttmacher, with Alfred C. Kinsey as a consultant) of the Group for the Advancement of Psychiatry, by a large number of states in the following decade and a half [*Note* 4]. Especially in those states that had maintained harsh penalties for sex offenses, the sexual psychopath laws may have been proposed as more "humane" alternatives to long prison sentences (Galliher & Tyree, 1985), and, to that extent, may have been perceived as "harbingers of a future in which all criminals would be *treated*" rather than merely incarcerated (Group for the Advancement of Psychiatry, 1977, p. 842).

Whatever their ideological origins, the laws of the various states differ from each other but little in their definitions of the criminal sexual psychopath or the habitual sex offender. Instead, these laws differ from each other primarily in assigning the responsibility for the execution of legislatively-mandated sanctions for the criminal sexual psychopath *either* to the public health authority, typically through a forensic psychiatric hospital, *or* to the correctional authority, typically through a specialized treatment unit resplendent with a staff of mental health clinicians (Glover, 1960). That difference in responsibility for provision of legislatively-mandated treatment is, of course, capital, since the pathways for release from the jurisdiction of the health authority differ markedly from the pathways for release from the jurisdiction of the correctional authority [*Note* 5].

Whose View of Sexual Psychopathology? And When?

These laws share the pivotal assumption that persons who commit sex offenses repetitively or "compulsively" are, presumably in some demonstrable way, mentally disordered *on that account alone* and thus merit sanctions that differ fundamentally from those to be applied to persons who commit the same offenses but *not* repetitively or compulsively. The history of the legislation appears to anchor in the notion of "sexual perversion," but only in the first case and not the second. Especially since many states had enacted sexual psychopath legislation prior to the codification of a commonly accepted lexicon of mental disorders via publication of the first edition of the American Psychiatric Association's *Diagnostic and Statistical Manual of Mental and Emotional Disorders* in 1952, it is not entirely clear what body of psychological or psychiatric knowledge was held to undergird that pivotal assumption. The language of the legislation differentiating two species of sex offenders is not particularly coincident with prevailing scientific views of psychosexual pathology, then or now.

The first edition of the American Psychiatric Association's *Diagnostic and Statistical Manual* (1952, pp. 38–39) is unequivocal in its definition of sexual deviation, nor does it admit of inflection predicated upon "repetition" or "compulsion" or "habituality":

000-x63 Sexual deviation
   This diagnosis is reserved for deviant sexuality which is not symptomatic of more extensive syndromes, such as schizophrenic and obsessional reactions. The term includes most of the cases formerly classed as "psychopathic personality with pathologic sexuality." The diagnosis will specify the type of the pathologic behavior, such as homosexuality, transvestitism, pedophilia, fetishism, and sexual sadism (including rape, sexual assault, mutilation).

No such diagnostic category survives in the current edition (Third, Revised) of the *Manual* (1987). Instead, sexual disorders are divided into the *dysfundions* (i.e., inhibitions in sexual desire or disturbances in psychophysiologic processes activated in sexual functioning) and the *paraphilias*, "characterized by arousal in response to sexual objects or situations that are not part of normative arousal-activity patterns" (p. 279). The latter continue to include exhibitionism, fetishism, frotteurism, pedophilia, voyeurism, transvestism, masochism, and sexual sadism. Though in common parlance rape and sadism might be equated, the *Manual* (1987, pp. 287–288) is quick to point out that "In most cases of rape, however, the rapist is not motivated by the prospect of inflicting suffering, and he may even lose sexual desire while observing the victim's suffering. Studies of rapists indicate that fewer than 10% have Sexual Sadism" [*Note 6*].
   The question of whether the offender is so mentally disordered (as a result, for example, of organic brain disorder or of profound schizophrenia) that he or she is unable to understand the requirements of the law in relation to sexual behavior or unable to conform his or her behavior to the requirements of the law is *not* at issue. In such instances, the offender would appear to meet the tests for an insanity plea and would subsequently be admitted on a criminal commitment to a forensic psychiatric hospital, so that the question of categorization as a felony sex offender rather than as a criminal sexual psychopath would not arise [*Note 7*].
   The question at issue in the implementation of sexual psychopath legislation, instead, is more primitive, and it might be formulated in such fashion as this: *When* is rape or pedophilia or some other variety of sex offense a "sexual perversion" and when is it "merely" a felony crime?
   If the answer is that such criminal behavior is *always* a sexual perversion, one is hard pressed to understand the sense of rectitude held to undergird the principle of differential sanctioning. And the weight of scientific opinion would seem clearly to fall on the *always* side of the ledger. *The implication legislatively and correctionally would seem to be that* either all or none *of those who commit sex crimes should be accorded the "differential" sanction of treatment.*

Homosexuality: From Deviation to Mere Anxiety

Changing fashions in the "acceptability" of sexual behavior of one or another sort in the general community and its designation as psychopathological, socially deviant, or merely normal within the mental health professions is perhaps best illustrated by reference to homosexuality. Consistent with the views of Freud and Krafft-Ebbing, not to say also with the strictures of most Western religions, the definition of sexual deviation just quoted from the 1952 edition of the *Diagnostic and Statistical Manual* is unforgiving in holding homosexuality in any form to represent a sexual deviation, and indeed the criminal codes of the various states contemporaneously proscribed such behavior [*Note* 8]. But, two and a half decades later in the exemplar *par excellence* of the politics of psychiatric nosology, homosexuality temporarily vanished from the official lexicon of mental disorders [*Note* 9], to be replaced in the third edition with the current "ego-dystonic homosexuality," in which the emphasis is placed on anxiety and depression resultant from gender preference (and typically arising from the reactions of others rather than from within the individual—that is, *extra*psychically and *inter*personally, not intrapsychically and intrapersonally), rather than from the fact of gender preference itself [*Note* 10].

Sadomasochistic heterosexual practices between consenting adults are today typically *either* not proscribed by law *or* not prosecuted criminally even when proscribed by law, except perhaps when the neighbors complain that the noise of clanking chains or lashing whips has disturbed their peace, not to say also piqued a prurient interest. Yet few mental health clinicians would fail to recognize a fundamental pathology in an exclusive devotion to such practices.

Since there obtains no strong congruence between legal and mental health definitions of aberrant sexuality, it requires no particularly fecund imagination to construct a variety of fairly comic scenarios in which the same behavior is at some times categorizable as both psychiatrically deviant *and* criminal, at other times as merely criminal but not as psychiatrically deviant, and at yet other times as deviant neither psychiatrically nor criminally. That state of affairs illustrates a clinical quandary of considerable proportions. Considerations such as these may have triggered Oliver's (1982–83) conclusion that "The mentally disordered sex offender is a purely legal categorization that has no meaning in psychiatry."

Calls for Repeal Largely Unheeded

Indeed, with the clarity of judgment that comes only with a quarter century of hindsight, the most recent report of the Group for the Advancement of Psychiatry (1977, p. 941) to deal with the topic, prepared by its Committee on Psychiatry and Law headed by the distinguished psychiatrist Carl Malmquist with the expert consultation of renowned criminologist Norval Morris, is neither so circular nor equivocal as its predecessor document, and it offers an opinion in diametric opposition to the earlier statement. The report categorically stipulates that "*Sexual psychopathy* is not a psychiatric diagnosis" (p. 840) and that "the term 'sex psychopath' ... is devoid of psychiatric meaning" (pp. 940–941), with the resulting recommendation that "*Sex psychopath statutes should be repealed*" (p. 940), largely, in the report's view, because they constitute an experiment that has failed either to control or to remediate socially deviant sexual behavior. In contrast to its predecessor document, which fostered the adoption of special sex offender statutes in a large number states, the GAP's latest statement seems to have had marginal legislative effect [*Note* 11].

During the late 1970s, a number of states (particularly those that had started life as European colonies and whose criminal codes therefore had grown by accretion since Colonial times) undertook to homogenize, streamline, and otherwise modernize their criminal codes. In such revisions, particular focus was placed on sexual behavior, since the earlier codes had surely not stopped at the door of the bedroom of consenting adults (Bienien, 1983; Borgida, 1981; Caringella-MacDonald, 1985, 1988; Sigler & Haygood, 1987); some proscribed not only "the unspeakable crime against nature," even between consenting adult homosexuals, but also a variety of behaviors by then commonplace between consenting and even married adult heterosexuals.

Given close scrutiny to legislation regulating sexual behavior on the part of the gubernatorial and/or legislative commissions empanelled to draft "contemporary" criminal codes presumably reflective not only of current community standards but also of scientific knowledge about the engines that drive aberrant sexual behavior, and despite the *absence* of support in the mental health community for a *continuation* of such statutes, it came as a considerable surprise that in virtually every instance the legislation governing the special treatment of criminal sexual psychopaths *survived* the revision of such codes. In so doing, the revisions perpetuated not only differential sanctioning patterns but also substantial inconsistency between legislative and scientific perceptions of sexual perversion [*Notes* 12, 13].

Notes

1. Biggs (1987) has provided a legislative history of rape law in Massachusetts, along with an interpretation of the sociopolitics of legislative change. The original legislation of 1642 prescribed death as the penalty for "carnal copulation by force and without consent" when the victim was under the age of ten or a woman "who was lawfully married or contracted," while the penalty meted out for the rape of an unmarried woman was left to judicial discretion. In 1692, the distinction between married and unmarried women was obliterated, but the death penalty remained as the legislatively-prescribed sanction until 1852. In related developments, the statutory "age of consent" was raised in the nineteenth century first to 13, then to 14, and finally, in 1893, to 16. According to Biggs, it was not until 1974, more than two centuries after the original enactments, that the law formally recognized *males* as prospective victims of rape.

2. For lucid analyses both of the *Coker* decision and of the social forces that led to the historic U.S. Supreme Court decisions of the last quarter century (preceding and following *Furman v. Georgia*, 1972, in which the Court ruled that the death penalty as then applied constituted "cruel and unusual punishment in violation of the Eighth and Fourteenth Amendments to the U.S. Constitution"), which collectively have all but led to the elimination of the death penalty for most offenses, see Zimring & Hawkins, *Capital Punishment and the American Agenda*, 1986, and/or Amnesty International's *United States of America: The Death Penalty*, 1987.

3. Dr. Vuocolo had a long and distinguished career at the intersection of corrections and mental health. At the time of his death, he was superintendent of New Jersey's Forensic Psychiatric Hospital and had been a long-term member of the Department of Corrections' Classification Review Board for Sex Offenders. Earlier in his career, he had been a social worker and psychotherapist at the Menlo Park Diagnostic Center, a unit charged with evaluating convicted sex offenders prior to sentencing.

4. Through the recommendations contained in its 1950 report on psychiatrically deviated sex offenders, the Group for the Advancement of Psychiatry, an organization of considerable leadership influence in the mental health professions, provided strong professional support in favor of then extant legislation. Specifically, although it opined that only "in the neighborhood of 5 to 10 per cent" of "males convicted of sex offenses" should be so designated, the GAP issued some eight recommendations for the criminal justice processing of psychiatrically disordered sex offenders, of which the most pertinent were: that there be evidence "of mental illness as diagnosed by expert opinion and as satisfying the existing legal definition of the same"; that psychiatric examination should be mandatory upon *conviction* for a sex offense and optional with the defendant even upon *accusation*; that, upon certification by psychiatric examination that a particular defendant should be classified as a psychiatrically deviated sex offender, commitment to a mental hospital "shall be in lieu of a sentence to a penal institution" if such certification is made following conviction and that, if such certification is made prior to conviction, "the diagnosis of a mental illness shall thereafter bar trial for the offense originally charged," although (quite inconsistently) "The court shall have the discretionary power to commit the convicted offender to a hospital facility in lieu of a sentence or to release the offender subject to special conditions of probation"; and that "Discharge shall be only upon approval of the court and under conditions generally governing release of mental patients" (Group for the Advancement of Psychiatry, 1950, pp. 3–4). Nonetheless, GAP was curiously equivocal in its definitional terms. GAP specifically eschewed the legal designation of sexual psychopathy then current (p. 1): "The Committee cautions against the use of this appellation 'psychopath' in the law ... There is still little agreement among psychiatrists as to the precise meaning of the term. Furthermore, the term has no dynamic [i.e., psychoanalytically interpretable] significance." Yet GAP's own definition is circular in the extreme: "The unlawful sexual act may be recognized as a surface symptom of a more profound psychic disturbance. In fact, the symptom may be less significant than other pathologic features of the total personality ... Thus it would appear that the psychiatrically deviated sex offender should be regarded as suffering with a mental disorder and that the procedure of disposition be by indeterminate commitment as provided by law for persons with mental illness." There is no effort in the GAP report to reconcile that circularity with what appears to be a speculatively, rather than empirically, derived estimate that only "in the neighborhood of 5 to 10 per cent" of those convicted of sex offenses should be caregorized as requiring mental health treatment. Perhaps it was considerations such as these that led "several members [to] oppose the

principle employed by current so-called 'sexual psychopath' laws," although GAP did not see fit to include a formal minority opinion in its 1950 report.

5. It is a quite predictable corollary that, in those states in which adjudicated criminal sexual psychopaths are confined for treatment under the jurisdiction of the correctional authority, some very large proportion (in some states, on the order of 50%) of all mental health professionals employed in the correctional system are assigned to serve only the very small proportion (rarely more than 5%) of all prisoners in the system—viz., only those who have been confined under the terms of such sexual psychopath legislation.

6. Szasz (1987, pp. 79–80) reports on the deliberations of the American Psychiatric Association which preceded the publication of the "third, revised" edition of the *Diagnostic and Statistical Manual*: "No doubt anticipating problems with newly discovered mental diseases like 'paraphilic rapism,' the psychiatrists invited several feminists to their meeting. The proposal that rape is a disease so upset the feminists, fearing that the diagnosis would provide an instant insanity defense for men who sexually assault women, that they threatened to sue." Szasz goes on to recount that, subsequently, the Board of Trustees approved inclusion of "Paraphilic Coercive Disorder as a new mental illness. With this diagnosis, the APA has taken another giant step toward psychiatrizing crime, since Paraphilic Coercive Disorder is, in fact, the Association's term for rape and other violent crimes that males commit against females." Whether as a genuflection to redundancy or not, however, this "new" category of disorder did not survive to see the light of publication in the current edition of the *Manual*. Szasz's summary comment: "Psychiatrists have, indeed, come a long way from the autocratic-Teutonic days of Kraepelin and Bleuler, when solitary … psychiatric investigators staked their reputations on claiming to have discovered new diseases."

Another "new" disease included in the current *Manual* (although only in a category labeled "proposed diagnostic categories needing further study") contrary to the predilection of the feminists is *self-defeating personality disorder*. According to Szasz (p. 80), this disorder "mainly afflicts women who stay in abusive marriages." Nonetheless, it is currently in wide use to describe what has been called "co-dependency" in relationships in which one partner is addicted to alcohol or drugs and in which the addiction is tolerated by the other partner. The implication is clear that the non-addicted partner is at least partly responsible for the behavior of the addicted partner. Since the non-addicted partner in such relationships is frequently victimized in one or another way by the addicted partner, inclusion of the new disorder in the lexicon of mental illnesses would seem to lay a firm foundation for psychiatrizing, in Szasz's sense, "the blame-the-victim" game, discussed in the succeeding chapter as an international pastime in the attribution of blame for criminal sexual behavior—but by no means limited to such situations.

7. It is a capital point to underscore, however, that the 1950 recommendations of the Group for the Advancement of Psychiatry, recapitulated in *Note* 4, *supra*, made no such artificial distinction between mere "perversion" and "insanity." Instead, it quite clearly held that persons to be sentenced to treatment as sex offenders should show evidence "of mental illness as diagnosed by expert opinion and as satisfying the existing legal definition of the same." Application of that stricture might be interpreted to require a judicial finding of *insanity* in a manner than runs sharply counter to the provisions of typical sexual psychopath statutes.

8. Nonetheless, the criminal codes of many states continue to proscribe homosexual behavior even among consenting adults, even if those laws remain largely unenforced; and it is to be anticipated that such legislation will continue to be challenged in the Federal courts on constitutional grounds in the future. In addition to adherence to traditional religious values, a variety of predictions of negative

social consequences are typically raised in discussions of whether homosexuality should be legislatively decriminalized. In Australia, which decriminalized homosexuality in the late 1970s, "the consequences of decriminalization did not include an increase in the negative aspects of homosexuality, such as public solicitation or sexually transmitted diseases," however. Instead, in a survey of adult male homosexuals, Sinclair & Ross (1985) reported that "Findings suggest that as a consequence of decriminalization the psychological adjustment of homosexual men will increase and sexually transmitted diseases and public solicitation will decrease ... there are few if any negative consequences of decriminalizing homosexuality."

9. The definitive social history of the political dynamics which led to the 1973 decision of the American Psychiatric Association to exclude homosexuality from the official lexicon of mental illnesses is yet to be written, though accounts in the popular press were voluble. Szasz (1987, p. 79) attributes the decision to "pressure from gay rights groups." Certainly the efforts of organizations representing the interests of gay men and women, then initiating pioneering struggles against discrimination on the basis of what has come to be called "gender preference," were potent. But it is likely that that decision also represented a sort of backlash against conceptual formulations of mental health and illness rooted in orthodox Freudian psychoanalytic theory. Best expressed in Freud's *Three Essays on the Theory of Sexuality* (originally published in 1905, and included in the Hogarth Press *Standard Edition* of 1953 at pp. 125–143, Volume 7), psychoanalytic theory had long held that homosexuality, whether among men or among women, represents an arresting of psychosexual development at a pre-adult level and that only heterosexuality is consistent with adult psychosexual functioning, so that even consentual homosexuality among adults is to be regarded as the manifestation of psychopathological disorder. As the Group for the Advancement of Psychiatry (1955, p. 6) put it in a remarkable document entitled *Report on Homosexuality with Particular Emphasis on This Problem in Governmental Agencies*, phrased in categorically unforgiving psychoanalytic terms: "Homosexuality is an arrest at, or a regression to, an immature level of psychosexual development." Freud's *Three Essays* had also in essence reduced the psychodynamics of women to envy of the penis, a notion that members of the women's liberation movement found as abhorrent as gay liberationists found Freud's notions of homosexuality. A more contemporary psychoanalytic view has been provided by Jortner (1985). Perhaps there lurked as well lingering resentment among the more scientifically oriented members of the psychiatric community about the over-reliance of the APA's earlier editions of the *Diagnostic and Statistical Manual of Mental and Emotional Disorders* (1952, 1968) on psychoanalytic formulations of mental health and illness generally, grounded as they are in elaborate and intellectually satisfying conceptualizations with but little empirical support which thus seem to many to constitute artistic rather than scientific creations.

10. As Szasz (1987, p. 58) has put it, in the American Psychiatric Association's lexicon, "homosexuality as such is not considered to be a mental illness; but *ego-dystonic homosexuality* (that is, homosexuality unwanted by the subject) is." At least among practicing clinicians, the midway reversal in adding *ego-dystonic homosexuality* to later editions of the American Psychiatric Association lexicon is understood as a function of the *economics* of mental health care. So long as a particular individual seeks professional treatment for a *recognized* mental disorder (i.e., one enumerated in the APA's official lexicon), his or her health insurance carrier has little choice but to provide reimbursement; removal of homosexuality in any form from the lexicon had the effect of permitting those carriers to deny claims for treatment when the diagnosis refers to a category that had been summarily eliminated,

however. To further illustrate the relativity of psychiatric nosology, in those nations that follow the World Health Organization's *International Classification of Diseases* rather than the American Psychiatric Association's *Diagnostic and Statistical Manual*, homosexuality has never "disappeared" as a "disease entity." Big as life, the disorder appears as "302.0, Homosexuality" (ICD-9-CM, 1989, p. 228) and is described as "Exclusive or predominant sexual attraction for persons of the same sex with or without physical relationship." With the 1989 decision of the Public Health Service of the U.S. Department of Health and Human Services to require that diagnoses be reported according to the World Health Organization lexicon in all Federally-aided health programs, it would appear to be the case that the same person would be labeled as mentally ill under the WHO rubric if he or she sought treatment, say, in a Federally-sponsored community mental health center or in a Veterans Administration hospital but would not be so labeled under the APA rubric were he or she to seek treatment from a private mental health practitioner.

11. California, the nation's most populous state, repealed its 35-year-old "mentally disordered sex offender" statute in 1982. Oliver (1982, p. 403) summarizes the principal differences between the current and former legislation: "Although the new laws do not entirely dispense with state hospital treatment of sex offenders, such treatment is no longer available as an alternative disposition at sentencing but as an option during the latter part of the prison term. The period of hospital confinement is limited to the term of the prison sentence and subject to the offender's amenability and cooperativeness to treatment." Forst (1978) summarized the legal bases for, and operational problems associated with, the commitment of sex offenders in California over much of the life of the original program.

12. The situation in the various states of the Union differs sharply from that of Canada, which in 1977 repealed its "dangerous sex offender" legislation, originally enacted in 1948 (Greenland, 1983, 1984). Substitute legislation created a "dangerous offender" category that included both repetitive sex offenders and other offenders who had repetitively committed crimes of violence; nonetheless, on the order of 75% of those sentenced under the substitute legislation between 1977 and 1985 were in fact sex offenders (Jakimiec, Porporino, Addario & Webster, 1986). In 1983, new legislation was adopted which "redefines rape from a sexual act to an act of violence, making it easier for rape victims to report the offense to the police and to provide testimony in court" (Renner & Sahjpaul, 1986). In some sharp contrast with developments in Canada, several states in Australia, which had originally enacted legislation concerning differential treatment of certain sex offenders (viz., homosexuals) as early as 1918, have within the last decade re-enacted and/or strengthened those provisions of their criminal sexual psychopath laws that govern the character of treatment to be accorded, especially to offenders who have victimized children (Glaser, 1988).

In the revision of the criminal codes in the various states in the late 1970s, it was often the case that sex offenses were collapsed into broader categories arrayed by severity of penalty assigned; indeed, such terms as "rape" have sometimes been replaced by descriptors such as "aggravated criminal sexual conduct." Giacopassi & Wilkinson (1985) have argued that such revisions have had the effect of further devaluing the victim and weakening the "secondary social control function of instructing the populace by defining socially unacceptable acts." Empirical analysis, however, does not appear to support such a contention. Loh (1981) found no change in the overall rate of prosecution and conviction even after legislative changes specifying degrees of culpability for sex offenses and concluded that "the main impact of the statutory reform has been a symbolic and educative one for the society at large, rather than an instrumental one for law enforcement."

LeBeau (1988) similarly found no significant differences in the rate at which sexual assaults were reported before and after revision of California's legislation.

Quite in contrast, however, Miller, Stava & Miller (1988, p. 186) observe that "After repeal of a Wisconsin statute permitting hospitalization of defendants convicted of sexual crimes, an increase was noted in the percentage of sex offenders among persons hospitalized after being found not guilty by reason of insanity, and a greater proportion of hospitalized sex offenders were diagnosed as not psychotic ... juries and judges in Wisconsin [more readily] accept the insanity defense in order to secure for sex offenders hospital treatment previously available under the Sex Crimes Act."

13. In some jurisdictions, the newly revised codes require an "impact statement" from victims of sexual offenses, along with recommendations from victims concerning the sentence to be imposed. In an analysis of the effect of these statements and recommendations on the decisions of sentencing judges in an Ohio jurisdiction, however, Walsh (1986) concluded that, while "this requirement may have a placebo value in that it creates the impression that something is being done," neither the impact statements nor the recommendations have a significant effect on the sentences imposed.

3 Criminally Deviant Sexual Behavior
Incidence and Sequelae

It is a relatively commonplace belief that the volume of sex offenses has increased markedly during the recent past. Whether such is the case, or perhaps merely an artifact of journalistic attention to sensational cases accelerated by "public awareness" campaigns, might be determined by review and analysis of information contained in such sources as the several *Sourcebooks of Criminal Justice Statistics*, massive annual compendia of data relating to crime and the operation of the policing, judicial, and correctional systems in the U.S. published by the Federal Department of Justice's Bureau of Justice Statistics (Flanagan & Jamieson, 1988; McGarrell & Flanagan, 1985).

The *Sourcebooks* condense a wide range of information drawn from reports of criminal activity from every law enforcement agency in the nation, along with data concerning police activity, judicial disposition in certain criminal cases, rates of incarceration in prisons and jails, probation and parole activity, and other indices of the size, complexity, and cost of criminal apprehension, adjudication, and sanction. Particularly pertinent to the present inquiry are data included in the *Sourcebooks* on the extent of victimization and on demographic characteristics of victims gathered from several studies published by the Bureau of Justice Statistics, even in the absence of formal reports to law enforcement authorities and in the absence of apprehension and prosecution of offenders.

Gross Data on Rape and Other Sexual Offenses

According to data recapitulated in the *Sourcebooks*, it is indeed the case that the number of episodes of attempted or completed *forcible rape* alone *reported* to law enforcement authorities had climbed in the quarter century between 1960 and 1985 from 9.6 per 100,000 inhabitants to 36.6 per 100,000 inhabitants, an increase of some 281%. By way of contrast, the rate of reports of all felony crimes included in the FBI's Uniform Crime Reporting Program had increased over the same period by only 186% and of all *crimes of violence* by 246% (Flanagan & Jamieson, 1988, p. 319). By way of context, the population had increased over the same period by only 32% (Bureau of the Census, 1989, p. 18). Certainly, the rate at which rape is *reported* to police has increased disproportionately both to the population and to the rate at which other crimes are reported.

Nonetheless, although the number of rapes and attempted rapes *reported* to police increased in the period between 1973 (the first year for which comprehensive data are available as a base) and 1986 (the last year for which comprehensive data are available), the number *estimated* to *have been committed*, whether reported or not, actually decreased (from 156,000 to 130,000), while the population increased by 11%; thus, the overall *number* of victimizations actually declined by nearly 30% over that period (McGarrell & Flanagan, 1985, pp. 316–317; Flanagan & Jamieson, 1988, p. 240; Bureau of the Census, 1989, p. 13). What appears to have changed significantly, then, is the *proportion* of the crimes committed which are *reported* to law enforcement authorities.

Further, forcible rape as defined in the FBI's Uniform Crime Reporting Program is far less than exhaustive of the total lexicon of behaviors legislatively defined in the various states as sex offenses. The FBI's definition includes only those instances of "carnal knowledge or attempted carnal knowledge of a *female* against her will ... regardless of the age of the victim," so that offenses in which the victim is a male (homosexual rape) and "Statutory offenses (no force and victim under the legal age of consent) are not counted" (McGarrell & Flanagan, 1985, p. 722). While these exclusions apply in respect of formal reporting of known episodes of criminal activity by law enforcement agencies, *victimization* studies are not bound by the lexical definitions of the Uniform Crime Reporting Program.

Other offenses clearly sexually aberrant in character, and inclusive of homosexual rape and incestuous behavior short of intercourse, are presumably "officially" reported by law enforcement agencies as episodes of felonious assault or as *other sex offenses*, with the latter defined, in somewhat quaint terms (that nonetheless reflect accurately the enormous variations in criminal codes from state to state, in a system of criminal justice that is frequently, and appropriately, described as a "Balkanized" state of affairs) as:

> *Sex offenses (except forcible rape and prostitution and commercialized vice)*: Included are offenses against chastity, common decency, morals, and the like, such as: (a) adultery and fornication; (b) buggery; (c) incest; (d) indecent exposure; (e) indecent liberties; (f) intercourse with an insane, epileptic, or venereally diseased person: (g) seduction; (h) sodomy or crime against nature; (i) statutory rape (no force); (j) all attempts to commit any of the above (McGarrell & Flanagan, 1985, p. 743).

Sourcebook data are far more comprehensive on episodes of forcible rape, included among the FBI's "index of serious crimes," than on "other sexual offenses." Inspection and collation of these data provide a broad overview of the extent of rape victimization in particular. As points of reference, it is useful to observe that Bureau of the Census (1989, pp. 15–18) data indicate that, in 1988, the U.S. population stood at some 246 million, with 49% of the citizenry male and 51% female; whites constituted 84% of the population and all non-white groups 16%. Against this background:

- The *Sourcebook* for 1988 estimates that some 130,000 episodes of rape and attempted rape occurred during the year under review, of which 50% were *not* reported to law enforcement authorities; somewhat curiously, a larger proportion of *attempted* rapes (53%) than of *completed* rapes (39%) were formally reported (Flanagan & Jamieson, 1988, p. 215).
- Some 83% of the cases estimated to have been committed, whether reported or not, involved a *single offender* [*Note* 1] and 17% represented cases of *gang rape* (Flanagan & Jamieson, 1988, pp. 228–230). An earlier *Sourcebook* had reported that 94% of the cases of rape and attempted rape involved a single victim, while 6% involved two or more victims (McGarrell & Flanagan, 1985, p. 302).
- Some 56% of the rape offenses involving a *lone* offender were committed by *friends, relatives, or acquaintances* and 44% by strangers; in contrast, in gang rape only 16% of the offenses involving *multiple* offenders were committed by friends, relatives, or acquaintances (Flanagan & Jamieson, 1988, pp. 230, 232). Only 27% of *completed* rapes but fully 63% of *attempted* rapes were perpetrated by strangers (*Ibid.*, p. 235). Such data may well explain the sharp differentiation in the rates at which attempted and completed rapes are reported to police.
- Some 51% of all rapes occur in one's own home or in the home of a neighbor or friend and 22% occur in such open spaces as streets, parks, or parking lots (Flanagan & Jamieson, 1988, p. 235); 36% occur between 6 p.m. and midnight, 24% between midnight and 6 a.m. (*Ibid.*, p. 234).
- In cases of rape or attempted rape actually *reported* to police, the rate per 100,000 of the population varies incredibly by state, with Delaware first with 86.9 episodes, followed by Alaska with 72.7 episodes, Michigan with 67.4 episodes, Florida with 52.7 episodes, and the District of Columbia with 52.4 episodes. At the other end of the spectrum, there were only 11.6 episodes per 100,000 of the population in North Dakota and 12.5 in Iowa (Flanagan & Jamieson, 1988, pp. 326–334). Since neither extent of urbanization, racial disparities in composition of the population, nor disparate ratios between male and female population suggest ready explanations (Bureau of the Census, 1989, pp. 23–26), these data seem to beg for interpretation by anthropologists rather than by demographers, sociologists, or psychologists.
- Against an estimate of 130,000 episodes of rape or attempted rape in a year and 84,000 formal reports of rape or attempted rape to law enforcement authorities, police made some 31,080 *arrests* for rape, as well as some 84,000 arrests for "other" sex offenses (Flanagan & Jamieson, 1988, p. 368), the specific character of which is not described. *Only 52% of all cases of rape reported to police were "cleared" by arrest (Ibid., p. 392); the*

ratio between the estimated number of rape victimizations and arrests is thus on the order of 4:1.

- Comprehensive data on the proportion of those arrests which result in conviction are not available [*Note* 2], since: "Although the Uniform Crime Reports and the National Prisoner Statistics programs provide nationwide data on specific law enforcement and correctional activities, no comparable uniform State and local judicial processing data exist" (Flanagan & Jamieson, 1988, p. 411). Nonetheless, the *Sourcebook* reports the results of a "pilot study" of the consequences of felony arrest in 11 states selected to resemble the nation in important demographic characteristics; collectively, the 11 states account for 38% of the national population and 37% of the episodes of *reported* crime (Flanagan & Jamieson, 1988, pp. 412–413). Among those arrested for rape, 76% were prosecuted and 50% convicted; among those convicted, 84% were sentenced to incarceration, 16% to probation or some other non-custodial sanction; among those sentenced to incarceration, 69% were given sentences greater than one year.

- If these proportions are reasonable estimates for the nation as a whole, one might expect that the 31,000 arrests for rape in a year (representing the 52% "cleared by arrest" of the 50% formally reported to police of all rapes and attempted rapes actually committed) to result in 23,560 prosecutions and 11,780 convictions, *so that the ratio between crimes committed and convictions is on the order of 11:1,* and in some 9,900 sentences to prison, *so that the ratio between crimes committed and the intrusive sanction of imprisonment is on the order of 13:1.* Among those arrested for "other sex offenses," the comparable ratios are that 87% of those arrested were prosecuted and 64% convicted; among those convicted, 73% were sentenced to incarceration, 27% to probation or some other non-custodial sanction; among those sentenced to incarceration, 45% were given sentences greater than one year. Nor do these data differentiate between those convicted offenders who are sentenced as felony offenders and those sentenced as criminal sexual psychopaths.

- The absolute number of *arrests for rape more than doubled between 1973 and 1986*, even though the absolute number of rapes estimated to have been committed declined by 17% and the number of rapes reported to police increased by only 27% over that period; similarly, the number of arrests made for "other" sex offenses increased by 125% over the same period (McGarrell & Flanagan, 1985, pp. 316–317, 464; Flanagan & Jamieson, 1988, pp. 240, 368). Males constituted 99% and whites 53% of all arrestees for rape; males constituted 92% and whites 78% of those arrested for "other" sex offenses (Flanagan & Jamieson, 1988, pp. 374, 376).

- *Prisoners incarcerated* for rape constitute 4.2% and those incarcerated for "other" sexual offenses constitute an additional 4.5% of the population of state prison systems (Flanagan & Jamieson, 1988, p. 494), but with no data provided differentiating what proportion of these were sentenced as *felony offenders* or as *criminal sexual psychopaths*, nor concerning the particular type of sex offense (e.g., heterosexual rape vs. incest vs. homosexual rape) for which these prisoners were convicted. Since in some states the latter group of offenders are confined under the jurisdiction of the mental health authority, it is significant to observe that Steadman, Rosenstein, MacAskill & Manderscheid (1988), utilizing data from a survey of admissions to state forensic hospitals conducted by the National Institute of Mental Health, reported that 3% of the nearly 32,000 admissions to these facilities in a year represent judicial commitments of *criminal sexual psychopaths* [*Note* 3].

• Among those imprisoned for rape, 69% had attacked white women and 25% black women; 30% of their victims were under the age of 18, 59% between the ages of 18 and 39; 47% of their victims were strangers; and 15% of the offenses involved multiple victims. Among those imprisoned for "other" sexual offenses, 78% had attacked white female victims and 18% black female victims; 74% of their victims were under the age of 18, 23% between the ages of 18 and 39; only 25% of their victims were strangers; and 20% of the offenses involved multiple victims (Flanagan & Jamieson, 1988, p. 252).

Intraracial Versus Interracial Victimization

It is a fair assessment to say that whatever fears the prospect of rape engenders are likely to be substantially increased as a function of racial difference between victim and attacker. Surely, interracial rape, and particularly interracial gang rape, attracts and sustains a disproportionate share of journalistic attention, especially when the victim or victims are white. *Sourcebook* data relevant to the issue of intraracial vs. interracial victimization indicate that:

• The estimated rate of rape victimization of persons over 12 regardless of gender is 60 per 100,000 of the *white* population, 120 per 100,000 of the *black* population, and 40 per 100,000 of the population that belongs to "other" racial groups (Flanagan & Jamieson, 1988, p. 222).

• Extrapolation suggests that 77% of the victims were white, 23% nonwhite, so that national data appear to indicate that the rate of *victimization varies from the distribution of races in the national population* in such fashion that non-whites (who constitute only 16% of the total population) are vastly "over-represented" among victims in relation to their proportion of the overall population.

• The estimated rate of rape victimization of persons over the age of 12 is 10 per 100,000 among *white males* and 20 per 100,00 of *black males*, 110 per 100,000 among *white females* and 200 per 100,000 among *black females* (Flanagan & Jamieson, 1988, p. 221–223). *There is no question that blacks, whether male or female, are at significantly greater "risk" than are whites.*

- Estimated rate of victimization varies substantially by socioeconomic class, such that the rate is 150 per 100,000 of the population among families whose annual income is less than $7,500 but only 10 per 100,000 of the population among families whose annual incomes is more than $50,000 (Flanagan & Jamieson, 1988, p. 225); the confounds between race and social class are too well documented to require further comment.
- *Rape perpetrated by a single offender against a single victim crosses racial lines relatively infrequently.* In such lone offender/single victim cases, 79% of the white victims in *attempted* rape cases and 82% in *completed* cases were attacked by white offenders; 82% of the black victims in cases of attempted rape and 87% in completed rapes were attacked by black offenders (Flanagan & Jamieson, 1988, p. 229). Similar arrays are not reported in cases of victims or offenders who belong to what Federal sources insist upon calling "other" races [*Note* 4].
- *Data on gang rape contrast sharply.* In cases involving multiple offenders and either single or multiple victims, 25% were committed by groups of offenders who were homogeneously white, 22% by groups of offenders who were homogeneously black, and 42% by groups of offenders of mixed races (*Ibid.*, p. 231).

As if to complement the comprehensive but rather general data reported in the *Sourcebook*, several investigations have studied victimization by race in sex crimes in more substantial detail. Thus, data on risk of victimization on the basis of race were analyzed in a study of all cases reported in a single year in Buffalo by Ploughman & Stensrud (1986), who assessed socioeconomic and demographic "risk factors in victimogenesis," concluding that *non-whites* were at greater risk than whites.

In a more elaborate study, LeBeau (1984) analyzed racial pairings between victim and offender in cases of rape in San Diego over a five-year period, finding that "rape is primarily intraracial during four years, but predominantly interracial during a fifth year" (p. 125). When he aggregated data over the five-year period, LeBeau (p. 136) reported that 58% of the cases represented intraracial pairings and that offenses *committed* by whites against victims of other races constituted 2.2% of the cases; by blacks against members of other races, 29% of the cases, with the preponderance (25% of the cases) against whites; by Latinos against members of other races, 11% of the cases; and by members of "other" races against victims not of their own race, 1 % of the cases.

One can also re-aggregate LeBeau's data according to *race of victim*. In this case, 53% of the rape offenses against white women in his sample were committed by white offenders, 33% by black offenders, 12% by Latino offenders, and 0.1% by offenders of "other" races. In contrast, 88% of the rape offenses against black women were committed by black offenders, 4% by white offenders, and 5% by Latino offenders. Only 36% of the rape offenses committed against Latino women were committed by Latino offenders, 23% by white offenders, and 38% by black offenders. Clearly, the *Latino women* in the LeBeau study *were at greatest risk for cross-race rape*, followed by white and black women, in that order.

Weapons and Resistance

Fears associated with rape assuredly accelerate at the prospect of assault by force-of-arms resulting both in sexual degradation and injury or death. *Sourcebook* data report that:

- In only 23% of the cases of rape or attempted rape were perpetrators perceived by victims to be armed with a weapon, with knives (53%) and guns (25%) as the typical instruments (Flanagan & Jamieson, 1988, p. 236).

An earlier *Sourcebook* had reported that some 88% of the victims used measures for self-protection, 89% of the time against offenders who were not armed (McGarrell & Flanagan, 1985, p. 311). Since weapons were *not* used in over three-quarters of the cases, it would appear that intimidation and/or threat of physical force is the *modal* instrumentality used by the offender to gain compliance.

Evidence from a study conducted by Silverman, Kalick, Bowie & Edbril (1988) at the Rape Crisis Center at Boston's Beth Israel Hospital may illuminate the specific circumstances under which weapons are and are not utilized. Subjects were 1,000 consecutive Center admittees, categorized as victims of "confidence rape" (i.e., those victims who had been raped by friends or acquaintances, 75% of the time in places where they had willingly gone with their assailants) or as victims of "blitz rape" (i.e., those raped by strangers, 63% of the time in a surprise attack in their own homes). In only 25% of the cases of "confidence" rape was a weapon used by the assailant vs. 54% of the time in "blitz" rape; the victim's life was threatened 49% of the time in the "blitz" situation vs. 35% of the time in the "confidence" situation. Nonetheless, the extent of resistance among "blitz" victims (67%) did not differ significantly from that of "confidence" victims (76%) in a relatively less threatening situation.

Several researchers have addressed the question of factors associated with victim resistance. As a general observation, Walker & Browne (1985, p. 179) have commented that women "are socialized to adapt and submit" to the instructions and demands of men, so that, during childhood, they do not "develop adequate self-protection skills, especially if they come from homes" with a high tolerance for the degradation of women. Burnett, Templer & Barker (1985), in a study of personality characteristics of victims who had been resistant or compliant to the threat of rape, found that resistant victims were characterized by a generally "fearless" attitude and that the absence of a weapon and a previous acquaintance with their assailants contributed to resistance. Levine-MacCombie & Koss (1986) and Amick & Calhoun (1987) reported similar findings in studies of victims who had successfully resisted "acquaintance rape."

In a study of resistance of victims in 41 attempted rapes and 95 completed rapes perpetrated by 72 offenders as inferred from official police accounts of these crimes, Quinsey & Upfold (1985, p. 40) found that:

> Victims were more likely to avoid being raped when they resisted, particularly when they screamed or yelled for help. There was no positive association between victim resistance and the probability of subsequent injury. Previous reports of resistance being related to victim injury [may mask the fact that] victims resist more strongly when they are being injured.

However that may be, there is scant comfort in the datum that, of the 136 victims studied by Quinsey & Upfold, nearly half sustained physical injuries *in addition* to sustaining the degradation of sexual assault, whether attempted or completed: two were murdered, 15 were seriously injured, and 50 were "slightly" injured.

Rate of Reporting Versus Rate of Committing

It has already been observed that the absolute number of rapes and attempted rapes declined by 17% between 1973 and 1986 while the population increased by some 11%, so that the *rate of victimization* for rape and attempted rape *declined* over that period by 30%. Over the same period, however, the number of *reports* of victimization made to police agencies increased by 27%, so that a smaller proportion of rapes and attempted rapes remained unreported. It is clear that the *number of reports* has accelerated while the *number of rapes committed* has declined; and it may be that some argument can be made in the direction of deterrent effect, with both the increase in reporting and the decline in rate of victimization likely attributable to changes in social climate.

Surely the last quarter century has been characterized by rapidly heightening awareness of criminal sexual behavior, attributable largely to the efforts of the women's movement. One need only consider the impact of such popular books as Susan Brownmiller's *Against Our Will* or of such popular films as *Lipstick*, of hot-lines, of crisis intervention centers for victims (Sharma & Cheatham, 1986), and/or daily journalism's voyeuristic preoccupation with the National Association for Man-Boy Love and the many and varied self-justifying publications attributed to that organization.

This period has also seen pervasive and well-organized campaigns aimed to stimulate reporting of episodes of sexual victimization of children carried out by the schools and by the child protective agencies in the various states (Randolph & Gredler, 1985; Reppucci & Haugaard, 1989), stimulated by (or perhaps eventuating in) widely-reported cases of wholesale sexual abuse by school personnel on both coasts (Shore, 1982), and formation of such self-help groups as Parents United for sexually abusive parents (Hunka, O'Toole & O'Toole, 1985; Pardeck & Nolden, 1985; Sagatun, 1982; Wolert & Barron, 1982). It is a reasonable speculation that such factors have congealed in such a manner that the *rate of reporting* has increased disproportionately to the *rate of committing*, so that a smaller proportion of offenses is today likely to remain *unreported*, precisely in consequence of such factors.

Reasons for not reporting an episode of rape or attempted rape cited in *Sourcebook* data include a belief that police "would be inefficient, ineffective, insensitive" held by 12% of the respondents to a National Crime Survey conducted by the Bureau of Justice Statistics who had been sexually victimized; an equal proportion feared reprisal from the offender; and fully 21% (perhaps those who had been assaulted by close friends or relatives) expressed the opinion that the episode of criminal behavior constituted "a private or personal matter." As an outrageous apostrophe as well as a judgment on the efficacy of the criminal justice system, only 17% of victims who had indeed reported victimization in completed rapes and 11% of the victims in attempted rapes expected the offender to be punished (Flanagan & Jamieson, 1988, pp. 217–219).

Several investigations have assayed the differences between groups of victims who do and do not report an episode of rape or attempted rape, either to law enforcement officials or to other public agencies. In a study of victims who had sought treatment at crisis intervention centers or other social agencies in Chicago, Peretti & Cozzens (1983) asked subjects to retrospectively reconstruct reasons for reporting or not reporting the episode formally. Their characterization of victims who failed to report (p. 84):

> These women found it difficult to accept the possibility that mere chance factors might have led them to be in the rape victim position. In essence, they seemed overly concerned with 'something' they had either done, or 'something' that they had failed to do, which might have been responsible for their being the victim of the rapist.

For these victims, *self-abasement*, whether precedent to or consequent upon the assault, is surely a governing variable. As if to provide validation across both cultures and legal traditions, Shaalan, El-Akaboui & El-Kott (1983), in a study of 729 victims of rape in Egypt, found that "reporting rape involved as much scandal for the victims as for the offenders, no matter how innocent the victims."

Two studies have been conducted in Seattle. Williams (1984) interviewed 246 rape victims who had contacted Seattle Rape Relief, a feminist rape crisis center, of whom 146 (or 59%, a proportion not grossly inconsistent with the *Sourcebook* figure for national data) had reported the assault to police. Based on information obtained through structured interviews, Williams found that it was *more likely* that the assault was reported when the assailant was a stranger, when the attack involved illegal entry or a chance encounter in a public place, when force was used or threatened, when the victim sustained injury, and when the victim sought medical treatment. In a more complex investigation, Feldman-Summers & Norris (1984) sought to differentiate victims who reported the assault to a social service agency from those who reported to police and those who failed to report to either. Their summary;

> perceived outcomes, social expectations, and situational characteristics of the rape [are] effective predictors of reporting or not reporting a rape. Specifically, women who reported to a social service agency were more likely than non-reporters to believe that reporting would result in tests to detect pregnancy, VD, etc., and would also result in a sense of psychological well-being ... Reporters were more likely to have been subjected to expectations to report by family members, friends, and/or spouse ... Women who reported to the police were more likely than those who did not to believe that reporting to the police would result in their being treated in a positive way by the police and that they would not have to testify in a trial. They were also more likely to have suffered [injuries] requiring medical attention and less likely to have been raped by an acquaintance [and had been] subject to stronger expectations to report by family, friends, and/or spouse ... Convincing rape victims [to report requires] efforts through the media, the schools, and any other useful channels to inform actual and potential victims that our social norms do in fact support the decision to report (pp. 569–570, 571–572).

Unfortunately, once the decision to report is made, there are other hurdles even before a formal investigation is launched, and here *victim characteristics* appear to play a major role. Rose & Randall (1982) studied the fate of some 610 reports of rape or sexual assault, with the finding that "victim credibility" represents a major factor in whether police investigators actually pursue a case through "full-scale investigation." In its turn, a judgment that the victim was credible pivoted not only on physical evidence and the results of medical examination but also on the investigators' assessment of the victim's "age, occupation, marital status, racial-ethnic group membership, and socioeconomic status," as well as "victim/offender relationship, circumstances surrounding initial victim/offender contact ... and resistance on the part of the complainant." Similar factors seem to operate in the assessment of credibility in accusations of incest (Weiss, 1983). Nonetheless, in a marvelously inventive study of the predictors and consequences of the decision of rape victims to participate in the prosecution of their assailants, Cluss et al. (1983) found that women who so decided had higher scores on a measure of self-esteem than those who did not at the point of their decision to prosecute and that *these differences accelerated* over the space of the year following that decision.

Blaming the Victim as an International Pastime

Whether social norms supporting the decision to report an episode of sexual assault and to undergo the travail of participating in the prosecution of the alleged offender in fact operate in real-world terms is another question. Edwards (1983) has argued convincingly that a generalized model of female sexuality, which holds in essence that women precipitate sexual encounters, supports notions like "contributory fault" and "negligence" both within the social climate and in the law and the formal operation of the criminal justice system. That model convincingly appears to influence how third-party observers assess the victim of sexual assault.

A substantial body of research evidence of international dimensions has demonstrated a generalized tendency for *women* cast in the role of third-party observers to *display greater sympathy for, and to attribute less blame toward, the female victim*, and conversely for men to display less sympathy and to attribute more blame toward the victim. In the typical experimental situation, observers are provided a variety of descriptions of sexual assaults, along with background information about victims and offenders, their past relationships, etc., sometimes with photographs; each variable is "experimentally manipulated" to increase or decrease the salience of certain characteristics. Respondents are then asked to judge to what extent blame should fall to the victim and/or to the offender.

The "blame the victim" effect, with male-female gender differences between respondents, obtains whether the respondents cast in the role of third-party observers were *college and university undergraduates in the United States* (Best & Demmin, 1982; Deitz, Littman & Bentley, 1984; Hall, Howard & Boezio, 1986; Karuza & Carey, 1984; Kraulewitz, 1982; Larmand & Pepitone, 1982; Mosher & Anderson, 1986; Pugh, 1983; Thornton & Ryckman, 1983; Thornton, Ryckman & Robbins, 1982; Wyer, Bodenhausen & Gorman, 1985); *or undergraduates in Canada* (Yarmey, 1985) or Germany (Smith, Tritt & Zollmann, 1982) *or India* (Kanekar, Pinto & Mazudmar, 1985; Kanekar & Vaz, 1983) *or Sicily* (DiMaria & DiNuovo, 1986); *or non-student citizens of Britain* (Howells et al., 1984; Sealy & Wain, 1980) or *Canada* (Yarmey, 1985); or, *more disturbingly, nursing* (Alexander, 1980; Damrosch, 1985) *or medical students in the United States* (Gilmartin, 1983), who might be expected to serve at some future point on the staff of crisis intervention centers; *and even among spouses whose partners have been victimized* (Earl, 1985).

This effect is especially strong when the experimental depictions suggest that the victim failed to take appropriate precautions (Pallak & Davies, 1982) or had herself consumed alcohol prior to, or during, the interaction that led to the rape attempt (Richardson & Campbell, 1982). In an astounding and particularly troubling finding, Deitz, Littman & Bentley (1984) reported that "subjects responded *least favorably* to an unattractive rape victim, particularly when she resisted the rape by fighting with her attacker." Apparently, not even behavioral science researchers are immune from the tendency to blame the victim. Thus, in a study that must surely have warmed the hearts of NAMBLA stalwarts, Ingram (1981) attributed responsibility for victimization in homosexual child abuse to "deprivation and family disturbance" and opined that "the children were none the worse off" because they had been criminally assaulted by adult gays; DeYoung (1982) attributed the "seductive behavior" of the victim of child sexual abuse to "pseudomaturity" on the victim's part; and Myers, Templer & Brown (1984) concluded that "rape vulnerability" was a product of psychosocial incompetence *on the part of the victim*. Even more disturbingly, in an analysis of the decisions of British appellate courts in cases in which the penalty for incest was at issue, Mitra (1987) found that "where the daughter was not a virgin, the court all but held her responsible." The underlying sexism is so rampant that it requires no interpretation [*Note 5*].

As one might expect, of course, the same effect is observed among rapists themselves (McDonald & Paitich, 1982–83; Scully & Marolla, 1984, 1985), so that it might be concluded, as Burt (1983) has suggested, that *offenders and the general public equally enjoy "blame the victim" as a pastime.*

One might be tempted to grimace sadly, shake one's head in disbelief, or do whatever one does when confronted with an unpleasant reality and try to suppress the evidence—were it not the fact that the respondents in these studies are, however remotely or proximately, *prospective jurors* in sexual assault cases. Indeed, there is some evidence that the "blame the victim" effect operates in the same way among members of criminal court juries as among "grab group" respondents presumably representative of the larger society. In their study of empathy toward both victim and offender among a sample of nearly 600 undergraduates and another of 170 jurors, Deitz, Blackwell, Daley & Bentley (1982) found parallel patterns and further reported that lack of empathy for the victim indeed influenced "jurors' ratings of defendant guilt and their recommended sentences for the defendant and their attributions of responsibility for the crime." Deitz and his colleagues interpreted their results in relation to "the low conviction rate for sexual assault cases and the importance of juror selection as a vehicle for increasing the number of just convictions." Relatively congruent results were reported by LaFree, Reskin & Visher (1985) in a study of the responses of 360 jurors who had served in rape trials to information about a victim's extramarital sexual behavior and its impact on their judgments of her assailant's guilt.

Some suggestion as to the fundamental dynamics around which the game of "blame the victim" pivots might be found in a study of Malamuth, Heim & Feshbach (1980) on the *sexual* responsiveness of college students to rape depictions of varying character. In sequential experiments, the investigators first determined that their subjects became more sexually aroused by depictions of consensual sex than by depictions of sexual assault. In the second experiment, the victim in criminal sexual violence was portrayed as experiencing an involuntary orgasm during the assault, with the result that this portrayal "disinhibited subjects' sexual responsiveness and resulted in levels of arousal comparable to those elicited by depictions of mutually consenting sex." Moreover, "female subjects were most aroused when the rape victim was portrayed as experiencing an orgasm and no pain" but "males were most aroused when the victim experienced [both] an orgasm and pain." Malamuth and his associates interpreted their results in relation to a belief common among rapists "that their victims derive pleasure from being assaulted." To judge by the universality of responses to the "blame the victim" situation, that belief is by no means limited to those who perpetrate crimes of sexual violence.

Psychosocial Sequelae to Victimization

Psychological and psychosocial consequences to victimization in rape, incest, and other forms of sexual assault have been widely studied by clinicians and researchers. There is general agreement that the short- or long-term sequelae include:

- *Abiding anger* (Owens, 1984; Price, 1985);
- An increase in *aggressivity* (Kutash, 1984);
- *Depression* (Becker et al., 1984; Ellis, 1983; Frank & Stewart, 1983; Resick, 1983; Santiago, McCall-Perez, Gorcey & Beigel, 1985) *and suicidal rumination* (Briere & Runtz, 1986; Ellis, Atkeson & Calhoun, 1982; Frank & Anderson, 1987; Kilpatrick, Best, Veronen, et al., 1985);
- *Drug and/or alcohol abuse* (Carson, Council & Volk, 1988; Covington & Kohen, 1984; Dembo, Dertke, et al., 1987);
- *Generalized experiences of fear, apprehension, and anxiety* (Calhoun, Atkeson & Resick, 1982; Ellis, 1983; Esper, 1986; Frank & Anderson, 1987; Girelli, Resick, Marhoefer-Dvorak & Hutter, 1986; Resick, 1983; Santiago, McCall-Perez, Gorcey & Beigel, 1985; Scheppele & Bart, 1983; Vernon & Best, 1983), especially in the presence of stimuli reminiscent in any way of the circumstances of the attack (Wirtz & Harrell, 1987);
- Feelings among victims that they were "worthless, undeserving, and helpless" (Van Buskirk & Cole, 1983) and/or powerless (Fine, 1983) so as to result in widespread *negative assessment of self-worth* (Carmen, Rieker & Mills, 1984; Carson, Council & Volk, 1989; Einbender & Friedrich, 1989; Lowrie, 1987; Owens, 1984; Scott & Thoner, 1986; Tong, Oates & McDowell, 1987; Verleur, Hughes & de Rios, 1986; Yates, Beutler & Crago, 1985);
- *Rape trauma syndrome* (Becker et al., 1982; Burgess, 1983; Colao & Hunt, 1983; DiVasto, 1985; Lenox & Gannon, 1983; Ruch & Leon, 1983);
- *Sexual dysfunctions*, including "inhibition of the psychological component of sexual responding" (Becker & Skinner, 1983; Becker, Skinner, Abel & Cichon, 1984; Becker, Skinner, Abel & Treacey, 1982; Ellis, 1983; Gruber, Jones & Freeman, 1982; Orlando & Koss, 1983) and continuing

problems in sex role differentiation (Cohen, Galenson, van Leeuwen & Steele, 1987; Kilpatrick, 1986; Roland, Zelhart & Cochran, 1985);
- *Sexual promiscuity*, both with opposite-sex and same-sex partners (Belcastro, 1982; Gundlach, 1977);
- *Social and work maladjustment* (Frank & Stewart, 1984; Resick, 1983; Resick, Calhoun, Atkeson & Ellis, 1981); and
- *Formal psychological or psychiatric disorders* of various sorts, including *schizophreniform psychoses* (Bryer, Nelson, Miller & Krol, 1987; Husain & Chapel, 1983; Varley, 1984), *depersonalization* (Coons, 1986; Coons & Milstein, 1984, 1986), and *somatization disorder* (Morrison, 1989).

Each of the symptoms cataloged can be construed clinically as related to the formal psychiatric disorder labeled *post-traumatic stress syndrome*; the current edition of the American Psychiatric Association's *Diagnostic and Statistical Manual of Mental and Emotional Disorders* (1987, p. 12; Brett, Spitzer & Williams, 1988) categorizes rape victimization as representing an "extreme" stressor in respect of this syndrome. The opinion of most knowledgeable mental health clinicians is that, while the symptoms of post-traumatic stress disorder can be ameliorated over time, the effects of the initial traumata remain life-long (Baum, Gatchel & Schaeffer, 1983; Feinstein, 1989; Frank, Kosten, Giller & Dan, 1988; Friedman, 1988; Hall & Hall, 1987; LaGuardia, Smith, Francois & Bachman, 1983; Malloy, Fairbank & Keane, 1983; Nezu & Roman, 1985; Stretch, Vail & Maloney, 1985; Zilberg, Weiss & Horowitz, 1982; *Note* 6].

Sadly, as Kilpatrick (1983, p. 35) observes, victims frequently "fail to conceptualize their problems as being victimization related." To provide professional mental health treatment for victims, women's shelters and rape crisis centers (Finn & Nile, 1984; Underwood & Fiedler, 1983) and a wide array of other organizations and modalities (Coates & Winston, 1983; Denham, 1982; Forman & Wadsworth, 1985; Herman & Schatzow, 1984; Holmes & St. Lawrence, 1983; Juda, 1985; Kelley, 1984; Lemmon, 1984; Lutz & Medway, 1984; O'Hare & Taylor, 1983; Plummer, Jenkins & Hampton, 1984; Raiha, 1983; Rodkin, Hunt & Cowan, 1982; Ruch & Hennessy, 1982; Valdiserri & Byrne, 1982; Yassen & Glass, 1984) have emerged to engage the task of what Bergner (1987) has aptly described as "undoing degradation."

Criminal Justice Sequelae to Victimization

Williams & Holmes (1982) argue compellingly that the effects of rape need to be reconceptualized as "an integrated composite of the public (extrinsic) and personal (intrinsic) experience of the victim." The psychosocial consequences of sexual victimization address only the personal or intrinsic experience of the victim, while the public or extrinsic experience includes not only both the reactions of "significant others" but also the manner in which the victim is treated by the criminal justice system. That is not always a pretty picture, so that Williams & Holmes might well argue that the process of victimization *continues* throughout the criminal justice processing of a formal report of victimization, so much so indeed that "the victim is often treated as if she were the offender" (Holmstrom & Burgess, 1975, p. 101; Holmstrom & Burgess, 1983).

Even so, case law and/or legislative action—frequently after successful lobbying campaigns by feminists and child welfare advocates—in many states has effectively modified the rules of evidence in offender prosecution, by limiting or eliminating the need for corroboration, through acceptance of uncorroborated testimony from child victims, and by holding as irrelevant the sexual behavior pattern of the victim or the sexual relationship between offender and victim prior to the episode of criminal sexual assault [*Note 7*]. It is reasonable to speculate that such forces as these have yielded a higher rate of *conviction* following arrest and prosecution than prevailed in the earlier period (Chappell, 1984; Myers & LaFree, 1982) and with more severe terms imposed (Beck, Borenstein & Dreyfus, 1986; Walsh, 1984).

Though not verifiable by reference to data of national scope on sex offense convictions inflected by type of offense and character of victim, it is a common impression among correctional authorities charged with operating treatment facilities that an increased incidence in convictions reflects in particular cases of homosexual rape and of child sexual abuse, including incest. *Sourcebook* data already reviewed on the age of the victims of prisoners incarcerated for "other sex offenses" (i.e., that 74% of their victims were under the age of 18) would tend to lend some fragmentary support to such an impression. Similarly, in a study of the severity of sentencing in some 166 prosecutorial jurisdictions over a three-year period, Champion (1988) reported that offenders who had sexually abused children were likely to receive harsher sentences than other offenders and were more likely to be incarcerated than placed on probation.

Despite formal changes, however, variables related to the credibility and the lifestyle of the victim continue to play major roles in criminal proceedings. Thus, McGaughey & Stiles (1983), in a study of the patterns of interrogation applied by prosecutors and defense counsel to rape victims in courtroom situations, concluded to intimidating tactics by defense counsel; and LaFree, Reskin & Visher (1985), in an investigation of the responses of jurors to information about the general pattern of victims' behavior, found that information about deviant behavior among victims indeed varied concomitantly with their judgments of credibility.

As Brant & Tisza (1977) have observed, the criminal prosecution process is usually particularly traumatic for child victims and their families. Poitrast (1976) and Greene (1977) have underscored a variety of impediments to proper judicial handing of child abuse cases, including the "real world" problem of lack of child care facilities into which victims may be removed from abusive family environments; similarly, Burgess, Holmstrom & McCausland (1978) have outlined the social-emotional disruption that ensues when incest is formally reported to law enforcement or child protective agencies. Schmitt, Gray, Carroll, et al. (1980), at Denver's National Center for the Prevention and Treatment of Child Abuse and Neglect, and Tyler & Brassard (1984) have urged uniform reporting procedures and uniform provisions for the protection and treatment of the alleged victim and provided sample protocols and guidelines. Weiss & Berg (1982) cataloged the consequences to victims of child sexual abuse of involvement in court proceedings, including delay in resolution of symptoms, intensification of extant problems, and addition of new stressors for children. Bauer (1983), Berliner & Barbieri (1984), Berliner and Stevens (1980), Elwell & Ephross (1987), Melton (1984), James (1989), Risin & McNamara (1989), Slicner & Hanson (1989), and Wakefield & Underwager (1989) have provided analyses of issues related to testimony from child victims, concluding with pleas that child victims in particular need to be protected from intimidation by either prosecutor or defense counsel. Empirically, the long-term effects on the child victim who is thus dually traumatized have been charted in the expected direction; it is thus quite likely that the criminal justice consequences of child victimization are such as to disincline the victim to expect in the future an orderly progression in the operation of the law.

Notes

1. The data apparently do not include cases of *conjugal rape*, however, except when these are formally reported to law enforcement authorities. Berk, Berk & Newton (1984) and Weingourt (1985) have underlined the barriers to disclosure of episodes of conjugal rape, including efforts to avoid dissolution of the marriage and fears that reports will not lead to official action by law enforcement authorities. Though a variety of fairly casual observations have opined that conjugal rape is a widespread phenomenon (Barshis, 1983; Finkelhor & Yllo, 1982; Frieze, 1983; Lystad, 1982), Hanneke, Shields & McCall (1986) put the overall prevalence of conjugal rape at 10% of all marriages and further observe that "sexual violence is almost always accompanied by non-sexual violence." Similarly, Truesdell, McNeil & Deschner (1986) found spouse abuse in 73% of families with a history of incest; Bowker (1983) found conjugal rape in 23% of the victims of *physical* abuse by their spouses referred to a marital violence clinic. In view of the finding by Groff (1987) that the wives of perpetrators in cases of father/daughter incest present psychological profiles on the Minnesota Multiphasic Personality Inventory generally within normal limits, failure to report episodes of personal victimization that have preceded, or are contemporaneous with, incest offenses becomes difficult to understand. In an observation that has the ring both of sexism and of truth, Earl (1985) asserts that the "victims" of conjugal rape indeed frequently at least implicitly consent. When conjugal rape is added, Reynolds (1984) asserts that the "true" number of episodes of sexual interaction that could be classified as forcible rape aggregate to something on the order of 4,000,000 annually. That astounding total would soar even further, however, if one accepts the methodology proposed by Russell (1982) in her survey of sexual victimization among a sample of some 930 randomly selected adult women in San Francisco. After reading the legal definition of forcible rape contained in California's criminal code, fully 44% of Russell's respondents reported that they had sustained at least one attempted or completed

rape during their lifetimes; but only 8% of these were reported to law enforcement authorities. Russell's conclusion: "Assuming that the prevalence of rape of females is not substantially different in San Francisco than in other major cities, the present survey reveals a problem of extremely serious magnitude ... the methods used by the National Crime Surveys to ascertain the magnitude of this problem should be radically overhauled because they yield incidence figures seven times lower than in the present study."

In an analogue study that has implications for the probable incidence of conjugal rape, Koss & Oros (1982) surveyed the sexual experiences of some 3,800 university undergraduates; fully 30% of the women reported that they had been subjected to physical force to grant sexual favors short of intercourse and 8% reported that they had been subjected to such force to engage involuntarily in intercourse; among men, only 6% admitted to the use of force to gain favors short of intercourse and only 2% admitted to the use of force to gain intercourse.

In a somewhat congruent finding, Finkelhor (1980) reported that 15% of the women and 10% of the men among the 796 university undergraduates he surveyed reported "sexual experience involving a sibling," in which "touching of the genitals was the most common activity." Clearly, such behavior constitutes sexual criminality of the incest variety, no matter how frequent or "normal" the activity of "playing doctor" may be during childhood (Burgess & Groth, 1980; Burgess, Groth & McCausland, 1981); and equally clearly such behavior is rarely reported to law enforcement authorities. Since both *Sourcebook* data and independent studies indicate that the rate of victimization in sex crimes is highest in the lowest socioeconomic strata and since it may reasonably be assumed that these strata are *under*represented among university undergraduates (i.e., that undergraduates are *not* randomly selected from among an age cohort), it may well be argued that the rate of sibling incest reported by Finkelhor constitutes a substantial *under*estimate for the population as a whole.

2. If the rate at which reports of rape or attempted rape "cleared by arrest" is 52%, what can be said of the likelihood of indictment, conviction, and incarceration or probation following arrest? To assemble data that respond to these concerns requires tracking individual cases through a number of pathways and into succeeding years: Criminal activity may be reported in one year, a suspected offender arrested and an indictment placed (or the charge dismissed) in a second year, and trial held (in consequence of various delays in preparation of the case, location of witnesses, and the like) in a third year. Although data which reflect the legal aftermath of arrest on suspicion of criminal activity are clearly of interest to legislators and framers of public policy no less than to the enforcers of law and administrators of justice, the relevant data are fragmentary and must be pieced together from a variety of sources to form even the semblance of a coherent picture.

The most comprehensive data of national scope on the varied possible sequelae to arrest are to be found in the several editions of the *Sourcebook* through 1980, though these rest on a source that, in social science research terms, can only be regarded as quite dated, *viz.,* the report of the President's Commission on Law Enforcement and Administration of Justice published in 1967. One wonders why, in the face of massive Federal expenditures in the bureaucratization of criminal justice statistics gathering and compiling since the passage of the "Safe Streets" Act of 1968, the matter of continuous sequential tracking of data bearing upon detection, apprehension, adjudication, and sanction has not become a routine feature of such activity; one might suspect, because the data might both indicate little positive change and prove rather depressing. Hence, however dated, the data from the 1980 *Sourcebook* constitute the most recent comprehensive Federal estimates.

These data reveal a framework that rests on what the President's Commission initially identified as a series of "funneling effects" between reports of criminal activity and imprisonment of adjudicated offenders, such that *indictments follow arrests in only 25% of all arrests for all episodes of "serious crime" reported, that 90% of all indictments result in conviction, that 40% of all convictions result in sentences to prison.*

Data reported in an earlier *Sourcebook* by Parisi, Gottfredson, Hindelang & Flanagan (1979, p. 545) from a major study of judicial practices in 1,334 courts in 19 populous states indicate a *median rate of guilty pleas of 86% in all indictments for serious crime.* In the absence of comprehensive national data from all U.S. jurisdictions, there is no particularly strong reason to believe that this rate varies substantially, whether positively or negatively, in the courts and states not studied. Similarly, data of national scope that speak to the extent to which the practice of plea-bargaining has preceded and produced so high a proportion of guilty pleas are not available. Indeed, empirical data on this practice have thus far been sparse and hardly revealing, a surprising state of affairs in view of what is assumed widely to be the universality of the practice. In some measure, the lack of responsive data may be explained by the finding that fully 69% of the criminal court judges responding to a nationwide survey of work styles in the courts reported that they were not aware of whether a plea bargain had been struck until the case actually came before them (Flanagan & McLeod, 1983, p. 110). The available data thus suggest that a plea of guilty represents the *modal* manner of disposition in criminal cases; judicial opinion supports the inference that some very large proportion of those pleas result from bargaining.

In these circumstances, final disposition of those cases in which a guilty plea is *not* entered is also of interest. Once again, responsive data prove fragmentary and incomplete but instructive nonetheless. Data concerning the final disposition in all criminal cases in a given year in two populous but dissimilar states, Florida and Connecticut, are reported by the U.S. Department of Justice's National Center for State Courts (1979, pp. 67–70) in a study of the operation of state courts. In all criminal indictments in which a final disposition was reached in the year under study and in which a plea of guilty was *not* entered, conviction after trial occurred in 13.8% of the cases in Florida and in 8.5% of the cases in Connecticut; conversely, charges were withdrawn or dismissed in 78.6% of the Florida cases and 85.8% of the Connecticut cases.

While extrapolations might prove interesting, the inescapable conclusions seem to be that *the overwhelming majority of criminal convictions almost certainly issue from pleas of guilty,* whether bargained or not, and that *proceeding to trial in the absence of a guilty plea is far more likely to produce withdrawal or dismissal of charges than any other result.*

But *how does this statistical mass illuminate what happens in the criminal justice aftermath to an act of criminal sexual violence?*

Expressed in primitive terms, the standard statistical method for estimating the probability of the *sequential* occurrence of two or more events hinges on the multiplication of the probability associated with the occurrence of one event by the probability associated with the occurrence of each subsequent event. On that basis, we can proceed to consider what the data just recited suggest in terms of the probability of apprehension, prosecution, and intrusive sanction for *forcible rape,* the single sex offense for which *Sourcebook* data are relatively complete. We must first make several questionable assumptions at which the statistical purist will surely blanch but which seem justified only because comprehensive national data are not available: That the rates of arrest and of indictment operate uniformly across individual episodes of rape (the most dubious of these assumptions), that the rate of indictment in cases of arrest is uniform across categories of crime, that the probability of conviction and the rate of imprisonment similarly operate uniformly across different individual offenders.

Under these circumstances, the arithmetic involved in the standard statistical formulae for combining probabilities works out this way: *In cases of rape, the rate of reporting to police agencies is known to be 55% and the probability of arrest after formal report to law enforcement officials is known to be 52%. Thus, we can expect subsequent indictment in 13% (i.e., 25% of 52%) of the cases reported, or 7% of all episodes committed (i.e., 25% of 52% of 55%) and conviction subsequent to indictment in 12% (i.e., 90% of 13%) of the cases reported or 6.3% of all episodes committed (i.e., 90% of 7%). Subsequent to conviction, we can expect sentence to probation in 7.0% of the cases reported (i.e., 60% of 90% of 25% of 52%) and sentence to prison in 4.7% of the cases reported (i.e., 4:0% of 90% of 25% of 52%). When the latter proportions are inflected by the committing vs. reporting ratio, they reduce to sentences to probation in 4% of all rapes actually committed and sentences to prison in 2.6% of all rapes actually committed.* In these circumstances, we might expect some 7,267 convictions to eventuate from 130,000 episodes of rape, of which 84,000 are reported to law enforcement authorities, and we might expect some 3,372 sentences to prison to result from those same 130,000 episodes of rape. We will be sadly disappointed if we search these data for evidence either of "just deserts" or of "deterrence."

3. Data of national scope are available neither on the *racial distribution* of those convicted of sex offenses nor of those convicted who are sentenced as "felony offenders" vs. "criminal sexual psychopaths." It is the widespread *impression* among clinicians affiliated with agencies and institutions that provide legislatively-mandated treatment for the latter, however, that the proportion of offenders committed for treatment who are white does not vary significantly from that of the national population. If that is indeed the case and if it is further the case that the race of the rape offender as perceived by the victim represents an approximation to the racial distribution of offenders in all sex crimes addressed by the mandated treatment laws, it would seem that race may represent a factor in the *type* of sanction imposed.

4. In this respect, the lone offender/single victim rape seems congruent with other types of violent crime that, as O'Brien (1987) has convincingly demonstrated, are primarily *intraracial* rather than interracial. More pertinently to the present inquiry, there are data that suggest *differential consequences* in criminal justice processing of sex offense cases according to race of the offender. Thus, Bradmiller & Walters (1985) reported that race is a potent variable in the determination of the severity of the charge entered at indictment, and Myers & LaFree (1982) found that "imprisonment was more likely when the defendant was black and the victim white." In a comparison of white and black victims of child sexual abuse, Pierce & Pierce (1984) found that black victims were more likely to have been abused at a earlier age, less likely to acknowledge the abuse, and more likely to remain at home following revelation of the abuse. In contrast, white victims were more likely than black to have been abused by their natural fathers, to fear that revelation would lead to family dissolution, and to have been abused by mentally disordered perpetrators. Overall, these findings were interpreted to indicate a higher tolerance for child sexual abuse among blacks. Similarly, Thornton & Carter (1986) have argued that "Society does not hold sexual misconduct among blacks to be of an equal degree of magnitude as that of whites ... when incest is reported in black families, it is often minimized or disregarded by agencies assigned to investigate and treat the problem."

5. Those historically inclined will recognize that the "blame the victim" turn of mind has an ancient history. In 1484, Innocent VIII approved publication of *The*

Witches' Hammer, the papal bull that set the Roman Inquisition in motion and which asserts categorically: "All witchcraft comes from carnal lust, which is in woman insatiable" (Summers, 1928, p. 47). The text continues: "There are three things that are never satisfied, yea, a fourth thing which says not, it is enough; that is, the mouth of the womb."

6. Nonetheless, state courts have ruled on the admissibility of expert witness testimony on the rape trauma syndrome and post-traumatic stress disorder in *Illinois v. Server* (499 N.E. 2d 1019, Illinois Appellate Court, 1986) and *Maryland v. Allewalt* (517-A 2d 741, Maryland Court of Appeals, 1986). Frazier & Borgida (1988) have discussed the role of expert witness corroboration that "an act of intercourse was not consentual" through evidence of persistent negative consequences.

7. With some minor modifications, the analysis of the sort of evidence admissible in sexual offense cases in British courts produced by the Royal College of Psychiatrists (1976) is applicable in the United States.

4 Clinical Inclusionary Criteria and Their Uncertain Application

Criminal sexual psychopath laws typically specify that the decision to so declare a particular offender (or, alternately, to declare him or her a "felony sex offender") is to be made by the presiding judge *after conviction* and *after, and in light of,* professional mental health assessment intended to guide that judicial decision. While that decision is a prerogative of the court, it is the clear legislative intent that the court's judgment be influenced by professional opinion that speaks both to the engines for the criminal behavior of which the offender has been convicted (that is, did the crime arise situationally or from "sexual psychopathy"?) *and* to the issue of future dangerousness. As earlier observed, in those cases in which an accused offender is so severely disordered that a plea of not guilty by reason of insanity prevails, disposition proceeds according to the pathway for involuntary criminal commitment to psychiatric hospitalization, without prior evaluation focused *specifically* on psychosexual pathology.

Brunette & Sales (1980) surveyed the legislation of all 50 states on "the roles of psychologists and psychiatrists in legislation governing sex offenders." Though not a principal focus of inquiry, their analyses yield a useful taxonomy of assessment methods and procedures legislatively mandated or permitted. Thus, in some states, the legislation prescribes that an offender *convicted* of a sex crime be referred for assessment to a specialized unit operated by whichever authority (health or correctional) is charged with providing treatment. In others, the offender is to be examined by three mental health professionals, one of whom is nominated by the prosecution, one by the defense, and a third appointed by the court. In still others, specification of the examining professional or professionals is apparently entirely a matter of judicial discretion. Implicitly or explicitly, the defendant has the right to challenge the recommendation of the examining mental health professionals as to whether he or she should be sanctioned as a felony offender or as a criminal sexual psychopath by assembling contrary evidence and submitting it to the court. Whether an offender may *waive* such examination and thereby opt for what is generally perceived to be the "harsher" punishment of incarceration as a felony offender rather than treatment as a sexual psychopath is a matter that varies substantially from state to state (Wettstein, 1986).

Clinical Assessment and Clear Empirical Referents

Clinical assessment in the mental health professions, as in medicine, generally proceeds in a relatively predictable fashion from the measurement of certain characteristics of the individual to the process of "fitting" those characteristics to patterns found among persons independently known to belong to one or another diagnostic category. Here, for example, are the "signs" that distinguish this individual (e.g., elevated temperature, hoarseness, mild nausea) at this point in time; how do they compare with the characteristic symptoms of those known to be experiencing, say, athlete's foot? German measles? Influenza? Technically, then, the process requires the specification of the extent to which the characteristics of the individual under assessment conform to, or deviate from, the empirically-validated *distinguishing* characteristics of members of diagnostic reference groups. In application, the process requires both sufficiently sensitive measuring devices *and* clear empirical referents to which measurements taken of individuals can be compared.

It is at that point that the mental health examination of the sex offender for purposes of differentiation into "felony" and "psychopathic" groups reaches a hurdle that has proven thus far virtually insurmountable—at least by means of the psychometric instruments customarily employed in psychological and psychiatric evaluation. It is a fair assessment to say that *there obtains as yet no commonly accepted, scientifically-anchored psychometric profile that differentiates the "felony" sex offender from the criminal sexual psychopath;* indeed, the available conceptual and empirical data are barely capable of differentiating the sex offender from non-offenders in general or from non-sex-offenders, let alone *between* categories of sex offenders.

General Conceptual Models

The task set for the mental health assessment of convicted offenders is to differentiate those who properly belong in the "guilty and mentally ill" category legislatively created for criminal sexual psychopaths from those who properly belong in the "guilty but not mentally ill" category reserved for "mere" felony sex offenders. Moreover, at least implicitly, mental health assessment should distinguish both these groups *from* those mentally ill offenders whose criminal behavior issued from non-focused, non-specific, generalized mental disorder. To borrow the characteristically incisive language of distinguished legal scholar Gerhard O.W. Mueller (1961, p. 204):

> An otherwise normal and responsive citizen may be a compulsive doorknob-wiper, a compulsive hand-washer ... [He] may be completely reality-grounded in driving his automobile or in doing other chores of daily life. He may meticulously stop at every stop sign and operate his automobile as a fully responsive and responsible traffic participant

... Yet [he nonetheless] may be a paedophiliac to whom the stimulus of the law means nothing in his relation to children. No threat of punishment, no reasoning can deprive him of his morbid urge to abuse children. He is as relatively free as you and I when it comes to filling out his income tax returns. But he is completely unfree in his sexual behavior toward children.

In short, the task imposed upon mental health assessment prior to sentencing is to distinguish such offenders as Mueller describes (i.e., those who suffer focused and specific psychological disorder, for whom confinement for treatment for *focused and specific sexual psychopathology* is the legislatively appropriate sanction, if any such exist) *both* from those felony sex offenders with no signs of criminally-relevant disorder (for whom imprisonment without mental health treatment is the legislatively appropriate sanction) *and* from those for whom intensive psychiatric hospitalization for *diffuse and non-specific* psychological dysfunction is the appropriate disposition.

A number of generalized conceptual models have been offered to account for the psychological dynamics presumably activated in criminal sexual behavior (Albin, 1977; Danto, 1985; Groth, 1979; Groth & Hobson, 1983; Knight & Prentky, 1987; Prentky, Cohen & Seghorn, 1985; Revitch & Schlesinger, 1989; Tollison & Adams, 1979), but without particular effort to distinguish such behavior according to the felony vs. psychopathy categories.

Despite many inventive abstractions, there is as yet little agreement about what engines drive criminally deviant sexual behavior. Indeed, the state of the discussion has not progressed significantly beyond the taxonomy of Cohen, Garofalo, Boucher & Seghorn (1977), who proposed a tripartite classification of the motives for sex crime as aggression, sexual satisfaction, or a diffusion between "sex and aggression ... in which sexual excitation is usually not experienced unless it is accompanied by violence"; or that of Groth & Burgess (1980), who proposed that the motives that underlie sex crimes are, respectively, "conquest and control, revenge and retaliation, sadism and degradation, conflict and counteraction, and status and affiliation," operating independently or in various permutations and combinations.

From the feminist perspective, rape in particular is seen as an act of aggression rather than sexual gratification (Alder, 1984) or as displaced "instrumental violence" for which women become more readily accessible targets (Van Ness, 1984), and criminal sexual aggression is held to result from the acceptability of violent male behavior toward women, supported by frequent depictions of their victimization in the mass and entertainment media (Briere, Malamuth & Check, 1985; Malamuth, 1986, 1988; Malamuth & Check, 1985; Marolla & Scully, 1986; Scully & Marolla, 1985). Nonetheless, at least one study by feminist psychologists concluded that "the evidence does not support hypotheses that characterize rapists as more hostile toward women than are other types of criminals" (Kozma & Zuckerman, 1983).

Psychometric Studies

Similarly, a substantial body of careful empirical research has investigated *ex post facto* a variety of psychometrically-inventoried psychological traits and characteristics of offenders *convicted* of one or another type of sex crime and sentenced *either* as felons or as psychopaths.

Not surprisingly, the most promising line of psychometric research has utilized the Minnesota Multiphasic Personality Inventory (a criterion-referenced self-administering test described by Clarkin & Hurt [1988] as "the most widely used assessment instrument in existence") in an effort to differentiate sex offenders from other offenders and from non-offenders. Thus, Rader (1977) found consistent elevations on that instrument's "psychopathic deviation" scale among offenders convicted, respectively, of rape, assault short of rape, and exhibitionism. Roughly congruent findings were reported by Anderson, Kunce & Rich (1979); Armentrout & Hauer (1978); Erickson, Luxenberg, Walbek & Seeley (1987); Forgac & Michaels (1982); Kalichman, Szymanowski, McKee, Taylor, et al. (1989); Kirkland & Bauer (1982); Hall, Maiuro, Vitaliano & Proctor (1986); Scott & Stone (1986); and Smith, Monastersky & Deisher (1987).

But, since this scale on the instrument is intended precisely as a measure of the propensity to behave in socially disapprobated ways—a task at which, according to distinguished psychologist Robert Hare (1985), the leading international authority on psychopathy as a general psychological characteristic, it continues to excel psychometrically—and, since the subjects in the relevant investigations had already been *adjudicated* as having so behaved, at bottom these findings come close to supporting Halleck's (1987) contention that *the diagnosis is redundant with the behavior itself.*

A substantial body of empirical data has yielded important information on a variety of variables that distinguish (however weakly in a statistical sense) sex offenders from those who commit other crimes *and/or* from those who are not offenders in any sphere. But the relevant research provides no dependable way to differentiate the criminal sexual psychopath from the felony sex offender. Thus, contemporary research in personality and social psychology has found sexual criminality, whether of the psychopathic or felony variety, to be empirically related to:

- *Abuse of alcohol* [Note 1] and/or other psychoactive substances (Beck, Boreristein & Dreyfus, 1986; Curtis, 1986; Pacht & Cowden, 1974; Vander Mey & Neff, 1984; Vinogradov, Dishotsky, Doty & Tinklenberg, 1988).
- *Deficiencies in heterosocial skill development* likely to result in feelings of heterosocial inadequacy and lack of assertive capacity in heterosocial situations (Baxter et al., 1984; Dutton & Newlon, 1988; Fiqia, Lang, Plutchik & Holden, 1987; Grier, 1988; Hobson, Boland & Jamieson, 1985; Howells & Wright, 1978; Lipton, McDonnell & McFall, 1987; Longo,

1982; Malmquist, 1985; Overholser & Beck, 1986; Ressler, Burgess & Douglas, 1983; Segal & Marshall, 1985; Smith & Monastersky, 1986; Stermac & Quinsey, 1986; Wydra, Marshall, Earls & Barbaree, 1983).

- *Deficiencies in the offender's sense of psychosexual identity* (Conte, 1985; Fisher & Howell, 1970; Freund & Blanchard, 1986, 1987; Giannini & Fellows, 1986; Greene, 1977; Longo, 1982; Malmquist, 1985; Panton, 1979; Scott, 1982).
- *Exposure to violence and/or violent pornography* (Comstock, 1986; Donnerstein & Linz, 1986; Goleman, 1985; Heath, Kruttschnitt & Ward, 1986; Linz, Donnerstein & Penrod, 1984; Malamuth & Briere, 1986; Malamuth & Ceniti, 1986; Sommers & Check, 1987; Smeaton & Byrne, 1987).
- *Dysfunctional family life* (Bidwell & White, 1986).
- *Impulsivity* (Panton, 1978; Prentky & Knight, 1986).
- *Personal sexual victimization earlier in life* (Becker, Kaplan, Cunningham-Rathner & Kavoussi, 1986; Burgess, Hartman & McCormack, 1987; Davis & Leitenberg, 1987; Fehrenbach, Smith, Monastersky & Deisher, 1985; Groth & Birnbaum, 1980; Herman, 1983, 1986; Kasper, Baumann & Alford, 1984; Malmquist, 1985; Petrovich & Templer, 1984; Pierce & Pierce, 1987; Seghorn, Prentky & Boucher, 1987; Tingle, Barnard, Robbins & Newman, 1986).
- Pre-existing *formal psychiatric disorder* (Coons & Milstein, 1984).
- A *generalized tendency toward aggression and/or hostility* (Burt, 1983; Coodley, 1985; Friedrich & Luecke, 1988; Greendlinger & Byrne, 1987; Hall, 1989-a; Johnson & Anderson, 1985; Kavoussi, Kaplan & Becker, 1988; Levin & Stava, 1987; Malamuth, 1986; McDonald & Paitich, 1983; Mosher & Anderson, 1986; Prentky & Carter, 1984).
- A *generalized tendency to view women as inferior* (Hall, Howard & Boezio, 1986; Koss, Leonard, Beezley & Oros, 1985; Murphy, Coleman & Haynes, 1986; Sattem, Savelis & Murray, 1984; Scott & Tetreault, 1987; Scully, 1988).
- A *generalized tendency to deny or minimize personal psychological dysfunction* (Lanyon & Lutz, 1984; Wysocki & Wysocki, 1977).
- *Seasonal variations in atmospheric temperature* (Bicakova-Rocher, Smolensky, Reinberg & DePrins, 1985; Michael & Zumpe, 1983-a, 1983-b; Perry & Simpson, 1987).
- In the case of incest, to *emotional distance between the victim and offender and between offender and spouse* (Groff, 1987; Groff & Hubble, 1984; Julian & Mohr, 1979; Money & Werlwas, 1982; Parker & Parker, 1986), to *authoritarianism in the offender* (Marvasti, 1985), and, especially in homosexual incest, to *tolerance of aberrant sexuality* on the part of the non-offending parental figure (Pierce & Pierce, 1985).

Many of these relationships, however, are reported as statistically weak and, further and in common with much research in personality and developmental psychology, later studies often contradict earlier findings. While these studies have contributed to an understanding of specific variables related to criminal sexual behavior, they have done little to illuminate the elusive distinction between felonious sex offenses and psychopathic sexual criminality.

To borrow Megargee's (1970) incisive formulation, the mental health community appears thus far to have failed to develop either conceptual or psychometric methods or models that reliably *post-dict,* much less *predict,* "psychopathic" criminal sexual behavior. In requiring mental health professionals to distinguish the felony sex offender from the sexual psychopath, at least on the basis of customary methods of psychological examination, the law thus appears to call upon mental health professionals to undertake a task for which there are sound and commonly accepted underpinnings neither in careful empirical research nor in theoretical formulations.

Psychophysiologic Reactivity to Sexual Stimuli

Despite occasional demurrers about the transferability of data from the laboratory to "real life" situations and/or the factitiousness of subject responses (Hall, Proctor & Nelson, 1988; Quinsey, 1973), the weight of evidence in a wide array of careful investigations (Abel, Barlow, Blanchard & Guild, 1977; Barnes, Malamuth & Check, 1984; Baxter et al., 1984; Baxter, Barbaree & Marshall, 1986; Davidson & Malcolm, 1985; Earls & Proulx, 1986; Eccles, Marshall & Barbaree, 1988; Freund & Blanchard, 1989; Freund, Watson & Rienzo, 1988; Hall, 1989-b; Hucker, Langevin, Wortzman & Bain, 1986; Madlafousek, Kolarovsky & Zverina, 1985; Malcolm, Davidson & Marshall, 1985; Marshall, Barbaree & Burt, 1988; Marshall, Barbaree & Christophe, 1986; Murphy, Krisak, Stalgaitis & Anderson, 1984; Pacifico & Brown, 1988; Quinsey & Chaplin, 1982, 1984; Quinsey, Chaplin & Upfold, 1984; Webster, 1980; Wormith, 1986) has rather convincingly demonstrated particular psychophysiological reactivity, as measured by penile tumescence (and/or by such other indicators as electrodermal activity and vasoconstriction, generally accepted as manifestations of anxiety and tension respectively), among sex offenders when exposed *in vitro* to aberrant sexual stimuli of various sorts.

Indeed, Quinsey, Chaplin & Upfold (1984, pp. 656), utilizing penile tumescence as the dependent measure, found strong evidence that *rapists differ markedly from offenders convicted of non-sex crimes not only in their responses to sexual stimuli but also to stimuli that depict non-sexual violence,* such that:

> [Stimuli] that involve vicious attacks and victim injury differentiate rapists from nonrapists ... Rapists [are] differentiable from nonrapists on the basis of their relative responsiveness to rape cues and consenting sex cues ... rapists respond more to rape stimuli than to consenting sex stimuli ... rapists respond to nonsexual violence involving female but not male victims ... non-sex-offenders' sexual arousal is inhibited by victim pain, whereas rapists' arousal is not ... [the sexual responses of]

non-sex-offenders are inhibited by descriptions of violence and victim injury, whereas [those of] rapists are not.

Those findings contrast rather dramatically with the weak psychometric evidence from studies that have attempted to differentiate sex offenders from other groups on the basis of those characteristics amenable to measurement by standard psychological instruments. They come close, indeed, to operationally specifying Mueller's (1961) prototypical citizen who may be law-abiding and tax-paying but "to whom the stimulus of the law means nothing" in relation to morbid sexual urges. And, while it may be the case that, as Kozma & Zuckerman (1983) have demonstrated, hostility toward women *as a generalized* and *psychometrically measurable trait* may not differentiate the rapist, his specific psychophysiologic reactivity to even verbal representations of violent behavior toward women most certainly does.

These studies, *which focus directly on behavior* or on the physiological substratum for behavior *rather than on the psychometric traits or characteristics which presumably underlie and/or dictate behavior,* would seem to lay a firmer foundation both for the diagnosis of pathological sexuality *and* for making the elusive differentiation between a felony sex offense and an offense that results from sexual psychopathy. Those offenders whose psycho-physiological reactivity is observed to vary from the norm in the direction of hypersensitivity to aberrant sexual stimuli would seem to fit the latter category, while an account that a sexual assault "merely happened" during the course of, say, a burglary, becomes more credible when the offender shows no particular sensitivity to such stimuli.

Few evaluative protocols, however, include such sensitivity measures, even though the weight of empirical evidence has shown such measures to be reliable and valid indicators of aberrant sexuality (Farrall, 1973) that meet the relevant legislative and judicial standards for "evidence" in criminal proceedings (Annon, 1988). As Pacifico & Brown (1988, p. 19) put it:

> It is very difficult, clinically risky, *and possibly negligent* to make diagnostic judgments concerning sexual offenders via clinical interview or psychological testing alone, yet for several decades this has been the case ... predictive validity increases along the following methodological hierarchy: (a) clinical interview only; (b) clinical interview and psychological testing; (c) clinical interview, psychological testing, and physiological evaluation.

Anomalies in the Neuropsychological Substratum

More fundamentally, the role of basic neuropsychology, neuropharmacology, and neuroendocrinology in violent behavior and in aberrant sexual behavior—whether behavior of either sort be adjudicated as formally criminal or not—is only now beginning to be understood. Scattered studies yield fragmentary evidence that coalesces to produce a picture that may be indicative but is not yet definitive.

A number of studies point toward *a prospective relationship between anomalies in neurochemistry and aggressive behavior, both general and sexual.* Thus:

- Several investigators (Bradford & McLean, 1984; Dabbs, Frady, Carr & Besch, 1987; Rada & Kellner, 1976; Rada, Kellner, Stivastava & Peake, 1983; Virkkunen, 1985) have reported *abnormally high concentrations of testosterone among inmates with a history of violent crime,* whether these were sexually focused or not.
- Whether such levels in fact dictate abnormal psychophysiologic reactivity to aberrant sexual stimuli is yet to be determined, but it would be remarkable were the statistical relationship found to approach zero. More pertinently to treatment or control considerations, testosterone levels are readily amenable to biochemical manipulation through hormone-suppressing agents that stop far short of "chemical castration."
- Among infrahuman species, animal studies have established linkages between *naturally occurring depletion of the neural transmitter serontonin and both aggression and increased sexual activity* (Feldman & Quenzer, 1984, pp. 248–252).
- In studies of violent offenders across types of crime, Matti Virkkunnen (1982, 1985, 1986) of the University of Helsinki has found evidence for the *abnormal metabolism of glucose,* an excess of which can produce "manic" states, especially among those diagnosed with antisocial personality disorder.
- Similarly, Boulton (1983), Davis et al. (1983), Lidberg (1985), and Virkkunen, Nuutila, Goodwin & Linnoila (1987) have found evidence of the *abnormal metabolism of monamine oxidase,* an important neural transmitter that regulates mood, the inhibition of which indeed constitutes the biochemical basis for many antidepressant psychotropic medications (Schatzberg & Cole, 1986, pp. 46–54), leading to the tentative conclusion of *an enduring relationship between impaired impulse control and naturally-occurring anomalies in the body's regulation of neural transmission* [Note 2].

Among a panoply of other findings that may *prospectively* be relevant to an understanding of deviant criminal sexuality, researchers and clinicians in neuropsychiatry and neuropsychology have produced evidence that:

- *Brain damage and/or neuropsychological deficit is significantly associated with high rates of violent criminal activity.* Thus, Blackburn (1975, 1979) found electroencephalographic (EEG) evidence of abnormally high cortical arousal among prisoners diagnosed as "primary psychopaths," and Howard (1984) similarly found EEG anomalies among violent offenders who had aggressed against strangers rather than against friends or acquaintances. Bryant, Scott, Tori & Golden (1984) reported consistent associations between neuropsychological deficit and a history of violent criminal behavior. Langevin, Ben-Aron, Wortzman & Dickey (1987), in a study that compared EEG readings, computer-assisted tomography (CAT) scans of the brain, and results of the Luria-Nebraska neuropsychological test battery, found "a consistent trend toward more neuropathology" in violent and assaultive offenders than in offenders who were guilty of property crimes; but, perhaps in a manner that explains weak statistical associations between inventoried personality traits and criminal behavior, these inventoried differences in neuropathology were *not* matched by differences in psychometric profiles on the Minnesota Multiphasic Personality Inventory.

- Gorenstein (1982) found evidence among subjects classified as psychopaths on behavioral and psychometric criteria of *dysfunction in the frontal lobe of the brain,* thought to be associated with such psychological functions as foresight, planning, and the regulation of impulses.
- More particularly, in an extensive investigation that involved both administration of a comprehensive neuropsychological test battery, measures of penile tumescence in response to erotic stimuli of varying character (male/female, adult/child), and CAT scans of the brain, Hucker, Langevin, Wortzman & Bain (1986) found *a high incidence of neuropathology,* particularly involving the left temporo-parietal region of the brain, *among subjects whose criminal histories classified them as focused pedophiles.*
- Most tellingly, Yeudall & Fromm-Auch (1979) found *significant neuropsychological abnormality in fully 96% of the sex offenders* they examined by means of sophisticated test batteries, with this finding confirmed by subsequent EEG readings. Similarly, at the Kessler Institute for Rehabilitation Medicine, Galski, Thornton & Shumsky (1989) found evidence of brain damage, or of significant neuropsychological dysfunction, in 77% of the incarcerated criminal sexual psychopaths they examined on the Luria Nebraska Neuropsychological Battery, discovering as well so strong an association between neuropsychological impairment and the degree of violence associated with the most recent sex offense that they were led to conclude that "the organic brain impairment discovered ... in this sample through neuropsychological examination establishes the link between brain dysfunction and aberrant sexual behavior ... violent sexual offenses seem to be linked with more severe neuropsychological dysfunction, specifically associated with left hemisphere functioning," thought to control (at least among those who are right-handed) such functions as sequential and analytic processing of ideas and concepts (Taylor, Sierles & Abrams, 1987, pp. 4–5).
- *The incidence of undetected and untreated closed head trauma,* likely indicative of brain dysfunction of at least a sub-clinical level of severity, *is*

substantially higher among members of lower socioeconomic status groups, among whom crimes of violence also show a higher incidence (Bell, 1986) and among whom, as *Sourcebook* data already reviewed indicate, rape is experienced with substantially greater frequency.

• *The incidence of epilepsy among prisoners incarcerated for criminal behavior of all sorts significantly exceeds that of control subjects matched for age* (Wettstein, 1987, p. 458). In a study of all new adult male admissions to the Illinois state prisons utilizing comprehensive neurological examinations, Whitman (1984) found the rate of epilepsy among prisoners to be *four times higher* than the incidence in a comparably aged group of non-prisoners and further attributed the probable cause of such epilepsy to undetected and untreated head trauma. Similarly, in Howard's (1984) sample of British prisoners, evidence of abnormal brain activity was found through EEG readings in nearly two-thirds of the cases.

• *Closed head trauma as well as injury or disease that yields damage to the frontal or temporal lobes frequently results in what is described as "pseudopsychopathic personality syndrome,* characterized by emotional lability (i.e., violent mood swings), socially inappropriate behavior, and hostility" (Stoudemire, 1987, pp. 134–135). Such traumata have been found to result in increased aggression, behavioral dyscontrol, impaired insight, and aberrant sexuality of various sorts, including hypersexuality, transvestism, exhibitionism, and fetishism (Wood, 1987, pp. 17–25).

• *Increases in sex drive typically follow injuries to the brain* that result in temporal lobe epilepsy, even of sub-clinical severity, such that "sexual behavior ... is usually marked by loss of specificity as to objects or forms of excitation" of such severity that "It is often helpful to make it clear to the family that the patient is not a 'sex maniac' when the patient's drives appear to become amplified due to brain injury" (Forrest, 1987, p. 394).

A Neuropsychological Etiology for Criminally Deviant Sexuality?

Given what is currently known about aberrant psychophysiological reactivity to sexual stimuli and what is either known or hypothesized about morphological structures in the brain thought to "control" impulsivity, aggression, and sexuality respectively [*Note* 3], and in light of at least fragmentary evidence about the incidence of anomalies in brain and brain-biochemical functioning among violent offenders, it may well be the case that future research will demonstrate conclusively that criminally aggressive sexual behavior results from disordered and very primitive neuropsychological or neurochemical processes over which the individual can be expected to exert little *volitional* control.

Some rather silly academic debates about antecedent and consequent conditions—concerning whether, for example, such personality traits as are measurable through psychometric or clinical instruments result from disordered neuropsychological processes or whether such traits (presumably acquired as the remnants of disordered developmental or learning processes) dictate disordered neuropsychological processes—might then be expected. But the modalities for "treatment" of sex offenders could surely be expected to veer sharply away from traditional psychotherapeutic "talking cures" and toward the neurosurgical and/or pharmacotherapeutic.

Should that state of knowledge arise in which convincing evidence is marshaled that criminally deviant sexuality is attributable to disordered neuropsychology as an antecedent condition, there will ensue a variety of other implications, as Wilson & Hermstein (1985, pp. 504–505) have somewhat satirically foreseen:

> If society should not punish acts that science has shown to have been caused by antecedent conditions, then every advance in knowledge about why people behave as they do may shrink the scope of criminal law. If, for example, it is shown that sex offenders suffer from abnormal hormones combined with certain atypical relations with their parents, then, by the existing standards of responsibility, why should their attorneys not demand acquittal on grounds of bad hormones combined with a particular family history?

Indeed; but some might expect to cheer, rather than lament, genuine advances in knowledge about why people behave as they do, whatever consequences may follow for the law, even such advances as may require society to radically reconsider its conceptions of responsibility, punishment, and deterrence.

Professional Assessment and the Criminal Record

In the light of a wide variety of unsettled questions concerning the engines for criminally aberrant sexual behavior, in the absence of widely accepted *empirical* criteria on which to base a *clinical* judgment as to whether such behavior arose situationally or stemmed from pivotal psychopathology, and with a shifting cast of actors among evaluating mental health personnel, one might well expect that the resultant professional assessments of which offenders should and should not be adjudicated as criminal sexual psychopaths could at best represent a heterogeneous grab-bag (Papen, 1988).

By whomever conducted and with whatever degree of knowledge and skill, it is a reasonable assumption that the typical evaluation comprises a developmental history, psychological testing, perhaps in a small percentage of cases also neuropsychological and/or neuropsychiatric examination, and, less often, psychophysiologic measures of reactivity to aberrant sexual stimuli. Implicitly if not explicitly, the evaluators are called upon to advise the sentencing judge as to whether the convicted offender behaved criminally *as a result of psychopathological compulsion or even of habit not reflected in the formal criminal record,* since determination of whether the offender acted *repetitively* would seem to be primarily a matter of enumerating prior convictions. As Myers (1965, p. 27) complained a quarter century ago:

> When an individual repeatedly appears before a court charged with the same type of offense, an opinion by an expert is relatively easy, for the behavior pattern speaks for itself ... Many examiners state that they know of no positive criteria of sexual psychopathy except a history of repeated acts, but many examinees are diagnosed [as criminal sexual psychopaths] on the basis of a single act and little else ... The law overlooks the uncertainty of diagnoses of sexual offenders and too often blindly accepts the opinion of the [expert].

Yet there is evidence that formal mental health assessment *in practice* merely recapitulates the formal criminal record. In his investigation of the variables on which mental health professionals relied in making recommendations to the court concerning whether an offender should be sentenced as a felon or as a sexual psychopath, University of Texas legal scholar George Dix (1976, p. 236) found that examinees

> evidenced very few of the traditional clinical symptoms associated with serious mental illness. *Consequently, the examiner's conclusions were often based primarily upon the defendant's past behavior.* Perhaps because of this reliance on prior conduct, the examiners seldom made any effort to address the psychological dynamics of the defendant's activities.

Further, an array of situation-specific variables that reflect the expectations of the offender might be expected to come into play during such evaluation. Has he or she been told by defense counsel, for example, that one can expect to do "easier time" in a sex offender treatment unit than in the general prison? What does he or she know of the greater likelihood of release from one sanction than from the other? And how do these variables interact when the interviewer asks, or fails to ask, "Even if you haven't been convicted of this sort of offense before, have you ever wanted to do it—or something like it?"

Clinical Influence, Redundancy, and Judicial Decision

In a study of factors that influenced the criminal sentencing decision in sex offense cases over a ten-year period, Traver (1978) found that judges followed recommendations contained in mental health evaluations on the order of 95% of the time, adding that "sex offenders who admit [to examining mental health clinicians] at least some involvement in deviant sexual activities stand a greater chance of being recommended" for less severe penalties, usually

probation rather than imprisonment (p. 403). Traver added, virtually incidentally, that only 12% of the cases examined met the criteria in California
legislation for classification as criminal sexual psychopaths (p. 410). However
that may be, and as if in counterpoint, in a report on California's "mentally
disordered sex offender program," George Dix (1976, p. 242), Vinson and
Elkins Professor of Law at the University of Texas, concluded that:

> no clear guidelines are available to clinical personnel for providing useful
> information to the courts. For sentencing purposes, past behavior pat-
> terns, progression from less to more serious crimes, and the circumstances
> of the present offense seem to offer clearer guidelines to recidivism than
> does clinical evaluation ... Clinicians offer no clear guidelines to the
> court on the high risk offender ... reliance on clinicians' opinions as to
> dangerousness is to be abandoned.

Though less directly, distinguished forensic psychiatrist Seymour Halleck
(1987, p. 83, with emphases added) similarly seems to advise reliance on the
verifiable behavioral record rather than on measurement of the psychological
characteristics of the offender in determining whether an individual should
be categorized as a felony sex offender or as a criminal sexual psychopath:

> States that still operate formal programs for the treatment of mentally
> disordered sex offenders have varied procedures for identifying them.
> Statutes differ in the criteria required to determine need for special treat-
> ment. Some states emphasize the requirement of a mental disorder or
> impairment. The type of disorder is usually not specified, except to note
> that it must be associated with or be the cause of dangerous behavior. Only
> a small number of those committed as mentally disordered sex offenders
> are psychotic ... *the sex crime itself appears to determine the diagnosis.*
> Certain patterns of sexual deviancy are part of the criteria for a group
> of disorders formally listed as Psychosexual Disorders in the third edi-
> tion of the American Psychiatric Association's Diagnostic and Statistical
> Manual of Mental Disorders ... An *individual who ... engages in these
> deviant behaviors may be automatically assumed to be mentally disordered.*

Assessment, Prediction, and False Negatives

The terms of that discussion—that is, reliance on professional mental health
assessment vs. relatively untutored inspection of the verifiable behavioral
record in the prediction of future behavior, especially of future "dangerous"
behavior—seem all too familiar.

Faust & Ziskin (1988) loosed a salvo of criticism in the pages of *Science*
about the validity of the forensic "evidence" offered by expert witnesses in the
mental health professions, contending that "professionals often fail to reach
reliable or valid conclusions" and that "the accuracy of their judgments does

not necessarily surpass that of laypersons." Though they do not claim specifically to address criminal sexual psychopath proceedings, their analyses derive primarily from empirical data related either to criminal cases or to involuntary commitment proceedings, and here they touch the tip of an iceberg that represents a monumental body of research on the *inaccuracy* of clinical assessment of future dangerousness and the clinical prediction of future violence.

That iceberg is so solid (Curran, 1975; Megargee, 1970; Monahan, 1976, 1981-b, 1983; Simon, 1987; Stone, 1976, 1984) that both the American Psychiatric Association (1974, 1984) and the American Psychological Association (1978) have taken official positions cautioning their members *against* predictions of future violent behavior [*Note* 4]. While not all mental health professionals are persuaded that the prediction of future dangerousness should be abandoned, often indeed for reasons of patient safety in mental hospitals (Barnard, Robbins, Newman & Carrera, 1984; Gunn, 1982; Hall, 1982; Litwack & Schlesinger, 1987; Skodol & Karasu, 1978; Yesavage, 1983) or inmate safety in prisons (Nacci & Kane, 1984; Swett & Hartz, 1984), and despite an early and comfortable assertion on the part of the Group for the Advancement of Psychiatry (1954, p. 6) about the relative ease with which the "deterrability" of criminal behavior can be predicted, the weight of empirical evidence clearly supports the "official" view of the two APAs [*Note* 5].

After reviewing the then-current evidence, Stone (1976), a prominent forensic psychiatrist, trenchantly commented that, since "mental health professionals, whether or not they use [actuarial] devices, simply have no demonstrated capacity to generate even a cutting line that will confine more true than false positives" and concluded that "a lay person can predict dangerousness at least as well as a professional." Monahan (1981-a), a distinguished psychologist-attorney, similarly concludes that "Psychiatrists and psychologists are accurate in no more than one out of three predictions of violent behavior over a several-year period among institutionalized populations that had committed violence in the past (and thus had a high base rate for it)," even though he observes that an unresolved, and perhaps insoluble, dilemma obtains between *"the patient's right not to be a false positive and the victim's right not to be set upon by a false negative."* Fersch (1980), another attorney-psychologist, is even more definitive:

> The laws ought to be changed. All references to psychiatrists and psychologists as predictors of dangerousness ought to be eliminated. Courts ought to discontinue the practice of requiring or even asking psychiatrists and psychologists for predictions of dangerousness [and] any predictions of dangerousness which need to be made ought to be made by lay persons within the court or correctional systems using the best available evidence, viz., the past acts of the individual in question.

Quite in contrast, Litwack & Schlesinger (1987) have reviewed a number of court decisions (beginning with *Tarasoff v.* Regents but including *Barefoot v.*

Estelle, argued before the U.S. Supreme Court in 1983 in a challenge to capital punishment) that have placed upon mental health professionals at a minimum the *duty to warn* those they have reason to believe are in "imminent danger" of victimization on the basis of information revealed by patients [*Note* 6]. Such a duty seems, in essence, to require that the clinician make a "prediction" of violence, albeit with the overt purpose of defeating that prediction (Hall, 1984). Nonetheless, renowned legal scholar George Dix (1983) has underscored the capital distinction between an assessment of *clear and imminent* danger to a *particular* prospective victim, as explicated in the *Tarasoff* decision, and a more generalized opinion about the prospect that a particular person, at some future time and under a specified set of conditions, *might* perpetrate a violent crime. As Dix puts it (p. 256):

> there is little reliable evidence verifying claims made by some members of the [mental health] profession of predictive skill. Such research as is available concerns mostly long term predictions concerning the conduct of persons without traditional mental illness; this research suggests minimal predictive skill ... psychiatrists' predictive ability is substantially greater when it is called into play concerning the short-term risk posed by persons whose assaultive tendencies are related to symptoms of identifiable serious mental illness. But claims of predictive skill even in these situations might be acknowledged to rest only upon intuition.

Without overly belaboring the point, one might speculate as to the rate of false positives and false negatives—not only in respect of the prediction of future dangerousness, but also in the sense of accurate and inaccurate categorization into "felon" and "criminal sexual psychopath" groups—to emerge from the evaluative process in sex offense cases dependent primarily on clinical interviews and psychometric instruments, particularly *in the absence* of data concerning psychophysiologic reactivity to aberrant sexual stimuli. The Group for the Advancement of Psychiatry's (1977, p. 940) stem dictum that "the term 'sex psychopath' is devoid of psychiatric meaning" and Oliver's (1982–83) conclusion that "The mentally disordered sex offender is a purely legal categorization that has no meaning in psychiatry" are entirely congment with Halleck's (1987) implicit argument that *the behavior itself is, or ought to be, redundant with the diagnosis.*

The nagging questions thereby raised need to be resolved in legislative or judicial chambers: If it is behavior rather than psychological characteristics measured *ex post facto* that is, or ought to be, the focus of assessment in pre-sentencing evaluations, and if a recommendation to sentence as a felon *or* as a sexual psychopath holds very different implications for post-sentence disposition, *why are not* all *persons convicted of sex crimes "automatically"* (in Halleck's sense) *classifiable as warranting confinement for treatment rather than for punishment?*

Notes

1. The relationship between sexual aggression and alcohol ingestion is likely not rectilinear—as it may be, in contrast, with certain central nervous system stimulants. That alcohol intake piques sexual interest but decreases sexual capacity, at least among males, was well known by Shakespeare's time. But contemporary research (much of it using penile tumescence as the dependent measure in relation to the ingestion of beverage alcohol vs. a "placebo") has demonstrated that, even among "social" drinkers (i.e., those who cannot reasonably be characterized as abusive in their patterns of alcohol consumption) with no history of aberrant sexuality, the subjective assessment of one's sexual capacity is not only not negatively affected by alcohol consumption but may indeed be accelerated thereby (Crowe & George, 1989; Farkas & Rosen, 1976; George, Dermen & Nochajski, 1989; Rubin & Henson, 1976; Wilson, 1977; Wilson & Lawson, 1976; Wilson & Niaura, 1984). Further, it appears to be the case that aggressivity is at least mediated, if not stimulated, by alcohol ingestion (Kelley, Cherek & Steinberg, 1989); and it may be the case that aggressive impulses link biochemically to sexual impulses in such fashion that the former potentiate the latter.

   Applying such findings to criminal sexual violence, Pandina (1989) sketches the following paradigm: A male perceives himself to be sexually deprived and therefore subjectively frustrated; he takes himself to a bar, both for the solace of alcohol and in at least the remote hope of finding a (perhaps willing) partner; upon a chance encounter, he perceives himself to be aroused to sexual capacity, though psychophysiological measures would suggest impaired capacity to perform; he approaches she who is soon to become the victim, but his advances are rebuffed; the rebuffing may lead to more aggressive advances; the experience of rejection leads to further ingestion of alcohol, interacting to yield both an increase in sexual interest and an increase in the capacity for aggression; at closing time, he accosts the rebuffer, and rather more aggressively; but, experiencing an inability to perform, he is administered a new dose of frustration; this experience yields, in the familiar paradigm, to an act of aggression, abetted to be sure by alcohol intake; *the experience of aggressivity restores sexual potency*, and an episode of rape is added to an act of aggravated physical assault. What is known about morphological structures in the brain that are associated with sexual performance and aggression, respectively, lends credence to Pandina's paradigm.

2. In an inventive multidimensional study that suggests the interaction of extrinsic forces and intrinsic neurochemical factors in the generation of violent behavior, Virkkunen, Nuutila, Goodwin & Linnoila (1987) observed a high rate of alcoholism among violent offenders in whom they had also observed anomalies in regulation of neural transmitters and opined that, because ingestion of alcohol represents a temporary corrective to abnormal metabolism of monoamine oxidase, "*alcohol abuse* in these individuals with a presumably deficient serotonergic system *may represent an effort to self-medicate*," even though "alcohol only makes the situation worse by further impairing impulse control." In other studies, Virkkunen (1983) has observed a relationship between abnormal metabolism of cholesterol and habitual violence *under the influence of* alcohol. Nonetheless, it will patently be the case that, whether at the scene of a crime or in later scholarly studies that rely on social history variables, violent behavior will be attributed to alcohol ingestion; the issue of why it seems to a particular abuser of alcohol that he or she "feels better" when drinking (i.e., the issue of whether alcohol use/abuse is itself *secondary* to a naturally-occurring neuro-anomaly) will scarcely be raised.

   More pertinently, Virkkunen, Nuutila, Goodwin & Linnoila (1987, pp. 245–246) appear to hold that even the present state of knowledge yields implications for the *pharmacotherapeutic* rehabilitation of violent offenders: "[Deficiencies in a metabolite of monoamine oxidase are] associated with aggression dyscontrol by being conducive of a heightened aggressive drive ... more specifically with a deficiency of impulse control and because of this with dyscontrol of intrapersonal and interpersonal aggression ... Aggressivity and impulse control problems are very closely related, especially in violent offenders ... In controlled clinical studies, both tryptophan and lithium carbonate have been found to be effective in reducing violent acts by habitually impulsive and violent offenders, and by adolescents with undersocialized aggressive conduct disorders characterized by severe aggressiveness and explosive impulsivity ... Thus, it seems that lithium carbonate may rather specifically ameliorate impulse control problems."

3. Though diagnostic categories like "organic brain syndrome" have long obtained, anything approaching a comprehensive neuropsychiatry and neuropsychology of mental health and illness has awaited the major technological advances in the neurosciences of the relatively recent past, as advanced techniques made it possible to record brain activity and later to map that activity through sophisticated imaging devices. A concomitant explosion of knowledge in psychopharmacology and psychoendocrinology has yielded new understandings of a panoply of interactions between brain morphology and functioning and emotional disorder. Thus, Harvard neuropsychiatrists Cohen, Buonanno, Keck, Finklestein & Benes (1988) have identified through CAT scans and magnetic resonance imaging consistent neuroanatomical anomalies in depressive and schizophrenic patients, even though "standard" neurological examinations had failed to detect these abnormalities in 63% of the cases they studied. At the neuroscience laboratory of the National Institute of Mental Health, Luxenberg, Swedo, Flament, Friedland, Rapoport & Rapoport (1988) have identified through CAT scans consistent neuroanatomical abnormality in patients diagnosed as obsessive-compulsive.

In a major review of the neuropsychiatric evidence concerning schizophrenia, the most insidious of the mental disorders, University of Maryland neuropsychiatrists Heinrichs & Buchanan (1988, pp. 16–17) conclude: "In spite of some methodological limitations, the evidence for a higher rate of neurological abnormalities in schizophrenia is consistent and compelling. These signs are not random but are concentrated in the functional domains of sensory integration, coordination, and sequential motor acts. There is some suggestion that these functional systems are impaired at the level of subcortical structures such as the limbic system. Furthermore, there are indications that neurological signs ... are more prominent among those with thought disorder and cognitive impairments, as well as those with chronic forms of the illness. In addition, there is significant reason to believe that neurological abnormalities characterize a portion of the relatives of schizophrenic patients and predate the onset of the schizophrenic illness." Since the vast majority of those criminal defendants who are found not guilty by reason of insanity are diagnosed as schizophrenic, the implications for forensic assessment are massive; perhaps also there are massive implications for societal constructs of criminal responsibility.

With particular focus on criminal behavior rather than diagnostic category, Hall & McNinch (1988) have summarized the current state of the evidence that links specific *neuroanatomical* (as distinct from *neurochemical*) deficits, anomalies, and impairments to specific categories of crime.

4. An American Psychiatric Association Task Force (1974) on the assessment of violence warned: "The state of the art regarding predictions of violence is very unsatisfactory. The ability of psychiatrists or any other professionals to reliably

predict future violence is unproved." For its part, the American Psychological Association (1978) similarly concluded: "The validity of psychological predictions of dangerous behavior, at least in the sentencing and release situations we are considering, is extremely poor, so poor that one could oppose their use on strictly empirical grounds."

5. In virtually all studies reported, the rate of "false positives" (i.e., those cases in which future violence is predicted, with restriction of liberty the likely consequence, but in which no future violence is observed) has been shown to be unacceptably high. Thus, in a carefully planned and executed series of studies of violence subsequent to release on parole among nearly 4,200 subjects conducted at the National Council on Crime and Delinquency's Research Center, Wenk, Robison & Smith (1972) found that a complex and putatively sound method of prediction that utilized both psychometric or actuarial, clinical, life history, and criminal history variables produced a *false positive* rate of 86%. Similar studies (Cocozza & Steadman, 1974; Holland, Beckett & Holt, 1982; Holland, Beckett, Holt & Levi, 1983; Kozol, Boucher & Garofalo, 1972; McDonald & Paitich, 1981; Menzies, Webster & Sepejak, 1985; Mullen, 1984; Rose & Bitter, 1982; Rubin, 1972; Steadman & Cocozza, 1978; Williams & Miller, 1977) reported false positive rates between 60% and 94%. In his review of the relevant findings, Monahan (1976) found the highest the "true" positive rate reported at 46% (with, reciprocally, 54% as the false positive rate) in an unpublished manuscript prepared by Maryland correctional authorities but not subjected to the scrutiny of peer review customary in scientific journals and thus suspect in the scientific community; no other study he reviewed approached even this level of accuracy, and several reached false positive rates between 94% and 99.7%. In a later analysis, Monahan (1981-a, p. 48) reported, almost incidentally, that those methods with the highest true-positive rates also produced the highest false-negative rates. In view of such data, it is hardly surprising that both the American Psychiatric Association and the American Psychological Association have cautioned against predictions of future violence.

To the contrary, however, Shannon (1985) has cogently delineated the differences between "risk assessment" and "real prediction." And Quinsey & Maguire (1986), in an inventive study of whether record of past behavior *or* the ratings of mental health clinicians better predicted the offense records of 360 inmates of a maximum security forensic psychiatric hospital 11 years after their release, found that *both* clinicians' ratings and subsequent offense records were associated with the number of previous correctional institutionalizations and the seriousness of the offense for which the inmate had been incarcerated. Quinsey & Maguire's clinicians had thus apparently learned to utilize the past behavior of the offender in making their own *clinical* predictions of future behavior. Yet, in a study of some 342 sexual offenders, Hall (1988) reported that, although "a linear combination of actuarial variables was significantly predictive of sexual re-offenses against adults ... clinical judgment was not significantly predictive of recidivism."

6. In *Tarasoff v. Regents*, the Supreme Court of California affirmed in 1976 that the psychologist who had treated an emotionally disturbed student at the University of California who admitted during treatment an intention to slay his former girl friend had a duty to warn the prospective victim and that this duty extended to the psychiatrist who had supervised the treating psychologist and to the Regents of the University, in whose name both were acting; in a 1980 decision in *Thompson v. County of Alameda*, the same Court articulated "the requirement that there be a readily identifiable victim before a duty to warn can be imposed" (Simon, 1987, p. 309).

In *Barefoot v. Estelle*, 1983, the U.S. Supreme Court upheld the Constitutional permissibility of the prosecution's use of expert psychiatric testimony that plaintiff (who had slain a police officer, apparently with premeditation and careful deliberation) would continue to behave in homicidally violent ways unless executed, despite a dissenting *amicus* brief submitted by the American Psychiatric Association recounting its earlier position paper on the prediction of future violence. Incredibly, the Court also held that such expert testimony "need not be based on personal examination of the defendant and may be given in response to hypothetical questions" (Amnesty International, 1987, pp. 217–218).

Weiner (1985) has reviewed a variety of issues related to duty-to-warn and to liability for inappropriate treatment with a specific focus on the treatment of sex offenders under judicial warrant.

5 Standard and Aggressive Methods of Treatment and Their Legal Constraints

Physicians customarily differentiate between therapeutic methods available for the treatment of a specific disorder as "standard" and "aggressive." Sequentially, "standard" treatments are typically applied first; if the patient fails to respond or the disorder persists, more "aggressive" remedies are applied. It may happen that a method of treatment that initially emerged as an "aggressive" remedy demonstrates such clear superiority in the treatment of a particular disorder that it is widely adopted as "standard." The focus in medicine is thus on the character of the disorder, and the aim of empirical medicine is to determine *which* treatments are likely to ameliorate *what* disorders—i.e., to identify therapeutic measures which are focused, disorder-specific, and disorder-effective and thus have been empirically validated as "treatments-of-choice" for specific medical disorders.

The mental health professions operate quite differently, prototypically with a focus on a "treatment method" proposed as very nearly universally applicable across mental disorders of various sorts, often on the basis of weak or limited clinical evidence and with little attention to what measures have been empirically validated as "treatments-of-choice" for which disorders, so that mental health therapy customarily progresses on the basis of treatment measures that are neither focused nor specific; nor is the distinction between "standard" and "aggressive" treatment modalities often made.

A dozen years ago, in a monograph published by the Department of Justice's Law Enforcement Assistance Administration, Edward Brecher (1978) of the American Correctional Association cataloged in some detail the regimens of treatment for offenders sentenced as criminal sexual psychopaths in some 28 programs nationwide. In the main, these programs relied heavily on traditional forms of "the talking cure"—group and individual psychotherapy, sometimes with a sex information and education component (MacDonald, 1971) and with substance abuse rehabilitation an optional feature in some. It is a fair characterization that the treatment modalities thus cataloged are essentially unfocused and non-specific, not to say also inoffensive and non-intrusive, and hardly capable of depiction as "aggressive" [*Note* 1]. Nonetheless, in view of their wide application, one might be led to conclude that these unfocused "talking cure" methods had been sufficiently validated empirically so as to establish them as "standard" and effective treatments-of-choice very nearly universally capable of yielding successful remediation of criminal sexual deviancy.

In what is surely a curious turn of events, however, little attention was paid in the Brecher report to the relative success or failure of these programs; instead, the monograph concludes with an appendix by noted criminologist Daniel Glaser on the difficulties of evaluating "successful" treatment of the criminal sexual psychopath [*Note* 2].

Standard Treatment Methods Largely Unevaluated or Ineffective

Nor is the phenomenon singular. Indeed, the most egregious gap in the literature on sex offenders is the virtual absence of carefully constructed, scientifically respectable outcome studies on the effectiveness of those therapeutic methods that represent the "mainstream" measures in legislatively-mandated mental health treatment for criminal sexual deviancy.

While some published reports detail the specific success of particular "experimental" programs (e.g., Dwyer & Amberson, 1985) and, doubtless, enumerations of success and failure have been produced in limited-circulation documents that detail on an annual basis the operations of those facilities charged with providing treatment under the relevant legislation in the various states, few large-scale investigations have been reported in the scientific journals and thus subjected to the scrutiny of critical scholarly review.

Hence, distinguished Canadian correctional psychologist Vernon Quinsey (1983, p. 36), though acknowledging that "there are many case studies and uncontrolled treatment studies that appear promising," specifically criticized the meagre studies available on methodological grounds, concluding that "There have been no convincing evaluations of treatment program efficacy." Nonetheless, Quinsey was able to generalize that "sex offenders who are treated ... with behavioral methods are less likely to recidivate than those who are not" [*Note* 3]. As Furby, Weinrott & Blackshaw (1989) have demonstrated, the same methodological criticism applies to studies of recidivism among sex offenders quite apart from considerations concerning the efficacy of treatment.

Similarly, in their survey of treatment programs for sex offenders both in the United States and Canada, Borzecki & Wormith (1987) complained of a virtual dearth of evaluative studies, published or unpublished, that meet reasonable scientific standards. One might wonder whether those responsible for treatment are simply so overburdened as to be unable to assess what it is they are doing—or whether, to borrow Stephen Vincent Benet's phrase, careful evaluation might engender the "burden of inconvenient knowledge."

One careful study that met scientific standards of respectability produced remarkably paradoxical results that surely yielded "inconvenient knowledge." University of Texas law scholar George Dix (1976) reported a seven-year follow-up of all California sex offenders sentenced a decade earlier. Of those who had been sentenced to imprisonment (i.e., as "felony" sex offenders), 7.3% had been convicted of a subsequent sex offense and none of a subsequent non-sex offense; of those who had been sentenced to treatment as "mentally disordered sex offenders" *and had been discharged from treatment as "no longer dangerous,"* 16.7% had been convicted of a subsequent sex offense and 12.5% of a subsequent non-sex offense. *The re-offense rate for sex crimes among those accorded the differential sanction of treatment was thus more than twice as high as that among those offenders upon whom the punitive sanction of imprisonment had been imposed.* In addition, those who had been "treated successfully" re-offended on crimes not involving sexual deviancy at a rate that exceeded the rate among those who had been punitively incarcerated at a ratio that arithmetically approaches infinity. Dix's understated summary, which may have contributed to the 1984 decision of the California legislature to repeal the state's sexual psychopath law:

> A sex offender treatment program may not be an effective method of reducing recidivism rates and (to the extent that it reduces the extent of "protective confinement" that would otherwise be imposed) may actually increase the recidivism of the participants.

Dix's stern conclusion is reflected, if not quite precisely echoed, by Furby, Weinrott & Blackshaw (1989) in the most extensive and meticulous analysis of the research literature on the effectiveness of treatment for sex offenders yet undertaken. Furby and her colleagues reviewed in detail some 57 studies reported between 1953 and 1987 (many issued only for limited circulation), excluding only those which dealt exclusively with offenders whose sole crimes involved consensual homosexuality, those which reported only single case studies, and those without specifically delimited follow-up periods. Several of the studies reviewed contrasted recidivism between offenders who had been "treated," whether under the aegis of health or correctional authorities, and comparable offenders who had not been treated, whether the latter had been punitively incarcerated or not. In none of the studies of "untreated" offenders was the rate of recidivism for subsequent sex offenses found to be higher than 12%. Although the rate of subsequent sexual re-offense varied wildly for studies of "treated" offenders (from a high of 40% among exhibitionists released as "no longer dangerous" in the 1950s from a California treatment facility to which they had been judicially sentenced to a low of 0% among exhibitionists treated in the late 1970s on an outpatient basis in Oregon), only 40% of these studies reported a recidivism rate of 12% or lower and fully 33% reported a recidivism rate higher than 20%.

More particularly, in the handful of studies analyzed by Furby, Weinrott & Blackshaw that precisely corresponded to Dix's investigation (i.e., those in which recidivism among sex offenders sentenced to treatment as criminal sexual psychopaths was directly contrasted with recidivism among felony sex offenders sentenced in the same jurisdictions to punitive incarceration), results almost precisely matched those reported by Dix—that is, the rate of subsequent sex crimes among offenders accorded the differential sanction of treatment was nearly twice as high as that among offenders accorded the punitive sanction of incarceration. With admirable scientific restraint, Furby and her colleagues identified (p. 25): "a general trend: The recidivism rate of treated offenders is not lower than that for untreated offenders; if anything, it tends to be higher." And, with the same admirable restraint, they concluded (p. 27), in virtually a precise echo of Quinsey's judgment: "There is as yet no evidence that clinical treatment reduces rates of sex re-offenses."

As if to add an exclamation point, in a ten-year follow-up study of convicted sex offenders *placed on probation* in Pennsylvania, Romero & Williams (1985) reported that only 11.3% had been *arrested* on a subsequent sex crime charge, with 55% of these arrests resulting in conviction, yielding a *re-conviction for sex offense rate* of 6.2% among sex offenders not incarcerated, whether for punishment or treatment.

Across these studies, then, one finds recidivism for sex offenses *lowest among probationers* and *highest among those offenders sentenced to the differential sanction of treatment*, with those punitively incarcerated in between. Even with full cognizance of a variety of differences (e.g., less severe offenses, less extensive prior criminal histories) that result in placement on probation, consideration of the differential costs associated with the provision of treatment vs. imprisonment vs. probation supervision enable these data virtually to speak for themselves [*Note* 4]: That is, if the legislation has been created to provide treatment specifically tailored to eliminate or reduce sexual psychopathy and if release from such treatment is predicated on a positive judgment of "improvement" or "cure," *why should one not expect substantially greater effectiveness from such treatment than from mere incarceration without treatment*—and on an order of magnitude that clearly justifies the greater expenditure of public monies for treatment than for punitive incarceration? If there obtains little convincing evidence that that expectation is regularly and routinely fulfilled, what possible rationale can support continuation of the differential sanction of treatment?

Aggressive Treatment Modalities

In contrast to the non-intrusive and unremarkable modalities cataloged in the Brecher (1978) monograph as constituting the core therapeutic regimens in those facilities specifically charged with providing legislatively-mandated treatment, more intrusive therapeutic modalities have empirically demonstrated very positive effect in the extirpation or control of criminal sexual deviancy.

In testimony before a Congressional committee contemporaneous with the publication of Brecher's catalog, distinguished correctional psychologist Nicholas Groth (1978) described a panoply of prospectively or demonstrably effective treatment modalities for "the dangerous sexual offender," including psycho-surgery, surgical and chemical (hormonal) castration, and behavior therapy, well beyond the usual regimen of group and individual counseling and sex education.

The Group for the Advancement of Psychiatry (1977) likewise enumerated a wide spectrum of treatment modalities, including behavior modification, psychosurgery, aversive techniques, surgical and chemical castration, and psychopharmacological behavior controls through medication, with rather detailed "risk-benefit" analyses for each. Similar catalogs, with only case-study evidence of effectiveness, were produced by Jadhav (1975) and Sadoff (1975).

Few of these more intrusive "aggressive" treatment modalities have been implemented in formal treatment programs for criminal sexual psychopaths in the United States (Beit-Hallahmi, 1974), however. And there is every reason to believe that a variety of judicial and legislative constraints in essence preclude their future implementation on a scale wide enough that they could be numbered among the "standard" techniques available for the treatment of criminally deviant sexuality in those institu-tions and programs charged with implementing the legislative mandate.

"Bioimpedance" Measures

Bloom, Bradford & Kofoed (1988) have utilized the term *bioimpedance* to denote a group of treatment modalities that aim at the control of deviant sexual behavior either through hormonal suppression by means of chemical agents, the use of various psychoactive medications to decrease impulsivity, or surgical or neurosurgical procedures to decrease sexual activity [*Note* 5]. British psychiatrist John Gunn (1976) and Canadian psychiatrists Bradford & Bourget (1987) have come very close to categorizing bioimpedance procedures as constituting collectively the "treatment-of-choice" in criminally deviant sexual behavior.

Chemical Castration

Bradford (1983), a leading Canadian forensic psychiatrist, has summarized nearly two decades of research evidence on the efficacy of control of deviant sexual behavior through the *pharmacological suppression of sexual drive* (by means of introduction into the body of hormone-suppressing biochemical agents, certain of which both affect the production of testosterone and appear to suppress aggressivity as well), in a treatment modality that could well be regarded as "hormonal castration," pioneered by distinguished psychologist John Money at the Johns Hopkins School of Medicine and in use in Belgium and other nations of Western Europe by the mid-1960s (Volcher, 1965). According to Bradford (p. 164),

> The various studies report positively that [pharmacological hormonal manipulation] causes a decrease in erotic fantasy, the frequency of erection and ejaculation, and [has] been beneficial in treating the paraphilias by causing a reduction in sexually deviant behavior.

Utilizing this technique, Bradford & Pawlak (1987) reported the successful treatment of sadistic homosexual pedophilia through administration of hormone-suppressing, aggression-reducing pharmacological agents. Wincze, Sudhir & Malamud (1986) reported similar physiological results in the treatment of pedophiles, observing as well that the treatment yielded a subjective decrease in self-reported states of arousal; and Cooper (1986) has concluded that such techniques, especially in conjunction with verbal psychotherapy, are particularly effective in treating "non-recidivist hypersexuals" who are well motivated.

Bradford (1983) is forthright in observing the prospectively negative medical side-effects of some agents used in pharmacological manipulation of sexuality. Neither he nor other commentators on the negative side effects of aggressive treatments for criminally deviant sexuality, however, address the negative consequences of *not* using such treatments, not only for the safety of future prospective victims, but for that of the offenders themselves, who may become the targets of "frontier justice" meted out by aggrieved parents, spouses, or lovers.

Surgical Castration

As one might expect, contemporary research on *surgical castration* as a treatment modality for sex offenders is sparse indeed. In a study of some 1,260 sex offenders who had been surgically castrated in West Germany, Langenluddeke (1965) reported a recidivism rate of 2.8% for sex offenses of any sort, commenting (in what must surely be a classic understatement) that this represented "a success rate which cannot be achieved by any other treatment method." In a parallel inquiry, 75% of the castrated offenders surveyed by Langenluddeke expressed neither ambivalence about, nor dissatisfaction with, this radically *extrusive* treatment modality; among the remainder, the opinion that this most aggressive treatment constituted "a crime against humanity" was not uncommon. Sturup (1972), recounting the Scandinavian experience in the application of surgical castration to some 120 sex offenders, reported a recidivism rate of 4.3% for subsequent sex offenses. Heim (1981) recited the subsequent criminal histories of West German sex offenders who had "agreed voluntarily" to surgical castration, with results similar to those reported for Scandinavia. And, in a report the authors labeled specifically as holding implications for the treatment of sex offenders, Rousseau, Dupont, LaBrie & Couture (1988) traced the effects on sexuality of variant treatments for prostate cancer through medically-necessary surgical castration vs. the equally medically-necessary administration of hormone-suppressing pharmacological agents resultant in chemical castration.

Two cases concerning the "voluntary" surgical castration of convicted sex offenders, separated by a continent and a decade, illustrate a variety of Constitutional, legal, and ethical quandaries in abundant detail. Brecher (1978, p. 52) recounts a situation in California in which social forces combined in such a manner as indeed to deny to the convicted offender the right to *choose* castration as an "heroically aggressive" treatment. Brecher's account, with some added emphases:

> In 1973, two 45-year-old sex offenders, both guilty of child molestation, *applied* to a California court for *voluntary* surgical castration. Both had been sent to Atascadero State Hospital for treatment. Both were subsequently returned to court with a finding that they were not amenable to treatment and were still "dangerous to society." The next stop would be incarceration in a California prison under the state's sexual psychopath statute. The period of incarceration would be indefinite, quite possibly for life with little or no possibility of parole. Faced with such a bleak future ... the men quite reasonably sought surgical castration with the likelihood that it might lead to parole. There were California precedents. Indeed, California courts approved voluntary castration on numerous occasions prior to 1968, when a civil suit brought by the American Civil Liberties Union against a judge and surgeon ... put an end to the practice. To get around this problem, the two applicants for castration in 1973 filed waivers releasing their lawyers, the judge, and the surgeon from any civil liability ... the case, interestingly enough, *was settled without regard for the interests or wishes of the two applicants for castration.* The surgeon who had initially consented to perform the operation if the court approved withdrew his consent following consultation with medical colleagues ... Medical Society officials [had] informed the surgeon that the legal waivers would protect him from civil suits by the men if they were castrated, *but that nothing would protect the surgeon from subsequent criminal prosecution* for mayhem or for assault and battery. Thus the two applications for castration did not fail because of any concern for the applicants *but out of a concern for the safety of the surgeon.*

A decade later, in South Carolina, the convictions of three defendants for aggravated gang rape (involving weapons, conspiracy, and kidnapping) raised even more troubling questions. Two defendants entered pleas of guilty, while the third was convicted at trial. The presiding judge in the court of first jurisdiction imposed on each defendant a prison sentence of

30 years, the maximum allowable under law, but added the condition that "upon each of you *voluntarily agreeing* to be castrated and upon the successful completion of that surgical procedure, the balance of this sentence will be suspended and you'll [*sic*] be placed on probation for a period of five years." Whether the "forced choice" conveyed in the judge's sentence could be construed as volitional in any real sense is barely debatable—but the case turned, not on whether the prospective castrations were construable as "voluntary" acts, but on whether the judge had the right to offer the option at all.

All three defendants appealed—but, while the case made its way toward the South Carolina Supreme Court, each decided to opt for castration-*cum*-probation rather than imprisonment. The state's Supreme Court nonetheless vacated the trial judge's sentence, ruling that castration is a form of mutilation and thus precluded by Constitutional guarantees against cruel and unusual punishment; hence, the "option" of "voluntary" castration was eliminated and the three were remanded for sentencing in accordance with statutory penalties. (See *State v. Brown, State v. Braxton, State v. Braxton, Brown, and Vaughn, 284 South Carolina Reports, Supreme Court & Court of Appeals*, 22235, 1984–85, pp. 407–411.)

In its risk-benefit analysis, the Group for the Advancement of Psychiatry (1977, pp. 904–905) somewhat grudgingly conceded that

> The effects of castration upon non-sexual criminal activity appear to be negligible. Castration appears to be a desperate measure consented to "voluntarily" by those who feel hopeless about controlling their sexual impulses in an open society where such behavior is not tolerated and otherwise leads to incarceration.

Anticipating the findings of Rousseau and his colleagues, GAP also noted scant evidence for *other* negative consequences to castration, whether in terms of mental health, physical health, or criminal activity, but was quick to add a value judgment masquerading as a criticism of research methodology:

> Questions are always prominent about how intensely an investigator is looking for adverse consequences … multivariate evaluation is exactly what is needed most and what is omitted in longitudinal studies concerning the effects of castration as a treatment for sex offenders.

One might add to that research agenda (phantasmagoric as it is, in the light of legal constraints on aggressive treatment modalities far short of surgical castration) the question of the number of *victims* who might not have become victims had society resolved to permit at least (or perhaps at most) *voluntary* surgical castration, especially when Groth, Longo & McFadin's (1982) estimate about the extent of victimization represented by *undeteded recidivism* is factored into the calculations.

Aversive Behavior Therapy

It is a fair assessment to say that, 25 years ago, before Federal legislation imposed a variety of strictures on such procedures through regulatory laws on "human subjects" in biomedical research and before the several landmark Federal court decisions that constrain treatment modalities in public hospitals and in prisons, clinicians active in the treatment of psychiatrically deviant sexual behavior (whether such behavior had also been adjudicated as criminally deviant or not) looked with great anticipation to *aversive behavior therapy* as an emerging, powerful treatment modality for sex offenders. That regimen proceeds largely through the process of *in vitro* "deconditioning" of the patient's aberrant responses to sexual stimuli or their photographic or symbolic representations.

Aggressive Deconditioning: "Treatment by Revulsion"

In the first edition of *Crime and Personality*, Hans Eysenck himself (1964) had perhaps set the stage by reporting in detail a combined regimen of mild electroshock and pharmacologically-induced aversion in the famous case of the "handbag slasher," for whom women's handbags and such related objects as children's perambulators had become "symbolic sexual containers" and who had undergone "many hours of traditional psychoanalytic treatment" without positive effect. Eysenck's account of the aversive treatment and its effects (pp. 169–170):

> It was explained to the patient that the aim of treatment was to alter his attitude to handbags and perambulators by teaching him to associate them with an unpleasant sensation instead of with a pleasurable, erotic sensation. Although he was frankly skeptical about the treatment, he said he was willing to try anything, for his despair had been deepened in recent sexual arousals when handbags appeared in the ward on visiting day and by illustrated advertisements in the newspapers. A collection of handbags, perambulators, and coloured illustrations was obtained, and these were shown to the patient after he had received an injection of apomorphine and just before nausea was produced. The treatment was given two-hourly day and night, no food was allowed, and at night amphetamine was used to keep him awake. At the end of the first week, treatment was temporarily suspended ... Treatment was recommenced [after eight days] and was continued as before, save that emetine hydrochloride was used whenever the emetic effect of apomorphine became less pronounced than its sedative effects ... Five days after the treatment had recommenced, he said that the mere sight of the objects made him sick; he was now confined to bed and the prams and handbags were continually with him, the treatments being given at irregular intervals. On the evening of the ninth day, he rang his bell and was found to

be sobbing uncontrollably. He kept repeating "Take them away," and appeared to be impervious to anything that was said to him. The sobbing continued unabated until the objects were removed with ceremony and he was given a glass of milk and a sedative. The following day, he handed over a number of photographic negatives of perambulators, saying that he had carried them about for years but would no longer need them. He left hospital but continued to attend as an out-patient. After a further six months, it was decided empirically to re-admit him for a "boosting" course of treatment ... Nineteen months after he had first had aversion therapy, he still appeared to be doing well. The patient reports that he no longer requires the old fantasies to enable him to have sexual intercourse, nor does he masturbate with these fantasies. The wife reports that she is no longer constantly worrying about him and about the possibility of police action against him. Their sexual relations have "greatly improved." The probation officer reports that the patient has made "very noticeable progress" and that "his general attitude to life, his conversation, and his appearance have all shown a marked improvement." As regards his work, he has been promoted to a more responsible job and he has not been in any trouble with the police.

During that early period, Raymond (1967) reported the application of what he called "treatment by revulsion," essentially parallel to the regimen of pharmacologically induced nausea coupled with electrical shock described by Eysenck, to other cases of sexually deviant behavior (fetishism, transvestism, exhibitionism) at Fairdene Hospital in Britain. But Raymond (p. 24) was insistent that genuinely effective treatment consists not only in eliminating undesirable (and/or illegal) sexual behaviors but in *substituting* for those behaviors others that are "normal," acceptable, and/or licit:

> aversion therapy in the context of sexual deviation consists of the use of conditioning techniques as a basis for psychotherapy. This aims to alter an individual's sexual behavior by teaching him to dislike, and to avoid, stimuli which he himself regards as abnormal excitants of sexual feeling. The fundamental principle of this treatment is that a sexual deviation is a learned or acquired pattern of behaviour. No matter how complex its elaboration has become, it is founded on a conditioned response established in early life ... In using aversion techniques, we are applying the method of extinction, which involves the learning of an alternative and unpleasant response to the deviant stimulus. The mere extinction of an abnormal sexual response is a negative result for the patient, though from the social point of view (particularly when there has been overt conflict with society and the law, or where the deviation has caused discord), it can be regarded as positive. To produce a normal sexual response is a more difficult and delicate matter.

Fookes (1969), a psychiatrist at Birmingham's Highcroft Hospital, reported "the experiences of five years of treating sexual disorders with behavioural methods," principally through aversive electrical shock upon presentation of pictorial sexual stimuli, with a success rate of 60% among homosexuals, 86% among exhibitionists, and 100% among fetishists and transvestites. In Manchester, Feldman, MacCulloch & MacCulloch (1968) reported treatment of cases of sexual deviation other than homosexuality through aversion therapy, with positive effects maintained at 16–24 months by fetishists and at 14–18 months by transvestite and sadistic pedophile subjects. At Netheme Hospital in England, Beech, Fraser & Poole (1971) successfully treated pedophilia, producing a transfer to normal adult heterosexuality, with the treatment effect maintained over the follow-up period.

At the Institute of Psychiatry at Maudsley Hospital, London, Marks, Gelder & Bancroft (1970) treated through electrical aversion transvestites and fetishists (with 67% "much improved" at 24 months' follow-up) and sadomasochists (with 60% "much improved" and 40% "improved" at 24 months' follow-up). Mac-Culloch, Williams & Birtles (1971) similarly treated adolescent exhibitionism in Birmingham.

In a study of patients with complaints of deviant sexual behavior, including pedophiles, homosexuals, and fetishists treated through electrical aversion at the Maudsley, Hallam & Rachman (1972) reported significant improvement in 60% of the cases. More pertinently, in a rare instance of hard evidence of the *internalization* and durability of therapeutic effect, Hallam & Rachman reported that aversive psychophysiological conditioning (measured through cardiac acceleration) had been *maintained* in relation to deviant stimuli over the follow-up period.

On this side of the Atlantic, Evans (1968) reported the successful treatment of exhibitionism through aversive electric shock in Toronto. In Vermont, Barlow, Leitenberg & Agras (1969) successfully treated pedophilia and homosexuality through covert sensitization. Serber (1970) reported the successful application of what he called "shame aversion therapy" in cases of transvestism, voyeurism, pedophilia, exhibitionism, and frotteurism treated at the Health Sciences Center at Temple University.

In the first issue of the British *Journal of Behaviour Therapy & Experimental Psychiatry*, Abel, Levis & Clancy (1970) reported the successful treatment of exhibitionism, transvestism, and masochism through electrical aversion at Iowa's forensic psychiatric hospital. In Canada, Reitz & Keil (1971) used *in vitro* desensitization to treat exhibitionism, with treatment effect maintained over a follow-up period of 19 months. With penile tumescence as the dependent measure, Callahan & Leitenberg (1973) contrasted aversive electric shock with covert sensitization in the treatment of exhibitionism and pedophilia in Vermont; although the methods were equally effective, positive treatment results were maintained during a follow-up period ranging from four to 18 months. In Ontario, Marshall (1973) employed a treatment regimen involving both aversion therapy and "guided orgasmic reconditioning" to successfully

treat pedophilia, fetishism, and homosexuality, with both attitudinal measures and penile tumescence as the dependent variables; positive effect was
observed in 92% of the cases at the conclusion of treatment and maintained
in 75% of the cases during a follow-up period of 16 months.

Behavior Therapy Integrated with Other Measures

A number of studies have combined the principal elements in aversive behavior therapy with other treatment measures. Woody (1973) reported the successful integration of aversion therapy with traditional psychotherapy in
cases of sexual deviation treated in Ohio. At the regional penitentiary in
Ontario, Marshall & McKnight (1975) introduced a treatment program for
inmates sentenced as "dangerous sex offenders" under then-extant legislation
that consisted of aversion therapy, social skills training, and a variation of
"milieu treatment," with positive post-treatment effects as measured both by
attitudinal questionnaires and by penile tumescence in response to aberrant
stimuli.

Wolfe & Marino (1975) similarly reported a successful treatment regimen
of ten weeks for violent pedophiles incarcerated at Connecticut's Sex Offender
Treatment Program that combined aversive conditioning to *inappropriate*
sexual stimuli, covert sensitization with hypnosis to *appropriate* stimuli, and
traditional group therapy, with 90% arrest-free at a ten month follow-up.
Recognizing that "The use of behavior modification techniques has ignited a
serious controversy of medical, legal, and moral dimensions" (p. 82), Wolfe
& Marino were quick to observe that each subject was permitted "to reach
an intelligent and knowing decision" (p. 76) on whether to participate in
the treatment regimen; a positive decision was reached, presumably know-
ingly and intelligently, by 93% of the offenders to whom the opportunity to
participate was offered, and "the men who refused participation, it should
be noted, were three time offenders," that is, those offenders for whom an
aggressive treatment modality might seem particularly appropriate, not only
for their own welfare but more particularly for their prospective fourth and
fifth victims.

While obviating many aversive elements common to these treatment regimens but otherwise utilizing the conceptual substratum that informs the
behaviorist canon, Laws (1980) successfully employed at Atascadero State
Hospital (the institution then charged with implementing treatment pursuant to California's mentally disordered sex offender act) a combination
of covert desensitization and biofeedback to remedy bisexual pedophilia.
In this regimen, arousal levels are inferred from such psycho-physiological
correlates of stress and anxiety as electrodermal skin conductance (measured by means of a psychogalvanometer) and vasoconstriction (measured
by means of peripheral temperature), with changes in these indices in
response to aberrant and normative stimuli directly readable by patient and
treater.

Similarly, in Montreal, Earls & Castonguay (1989) successfully incorporated noxious *olfactory* stimuli in the aversive treatment of bisexual pedophilia. Such other clinicians as Lang, Lloyd & Fiqia (1985) sought to incorporate interventions such as *goal setting* and *behavioral contracting* from the repertoire of behavior therapy into the "standard" talking cure programs, and Swan, Press & Briggs (1985) adapted elements related to *learning through social imitation* to efforts to prevent the sexual abuse of children.

"Psychiatric Seclusion"

To facilitate treatment for "patients who have remained untouched by other forms of therapy and for whom a major personality alteration may be the only means of avoiding lifelong incarceration," Canadian psychiatrists Barker & McLaughlin (1977) designed a "total encounter capsule" to ensure "sensory deprivation in psychiatric seclusion" (Grassian & Friedman, 1986) as a catalyst to aggressive treatment sure to gladden the hearts of more than a few old-line corrections personnel. Barker & McLaughlin's (p. 355) description:

> a specially constructed, soundproof, windowless but continuously lighted and ventilated room, 8 by 10 feet, which provides the basic essentials (liquid food dispensers, washing and toilet facilities) and in which it is possible for ... patients to live for many days at a time, totally removed from contact with the outside ... to the exclusion of distractions ... Participants wear no clothing ... In the first six months of the capsule's nine years of use, 90% of the participants reported that it led to ... a better knowledge about how one individual affects another.

A Treatment-of-Choice?

In contrast to those traditional, unfocused, non-specific (and largely barely intrusive) forms of "talking cure" mental health treatment that aim at inducing greater "behavior control" as a sort of by-product of increased insight into the engines that drive one's behavior (Shorts, 1985), the methods of treatment utilized in these investigations measured aberrant sexual behavior rather directly, often indeed employing penile tumescence as a principal criterion index.

The evidence had accumulated at such rate and in such direction that, by the early 1970s, it seemed to be the case that *aversive behavior therapy*, especially as aided pharmacologically to induce negative physiologic responses to aberrant *in vitro* stimuli but generally without the relatively "more" intrusive inclusion of pharmacological agents that alter hormone production so as to induce "chemical castration," *had virtually established itself as the treatment-of-choice for aggressive sexual deviation* (Barlow, 1973; Moss, Rada & Appel, 1970; Quinsey, 1973; Rachman & Teasdale, 1969), if not quite yet as the treatment-of-choice for *criminal* sexual deviation. As Marshall (1973, p. 557) put it:

> Aversion therapy of one sort or another has been the main, if not the only, component of most successful behavioral treatment methods aimed at reducing the frequency of deviant sexual behaviors.

Adverse Public Reaction: the Chaplain's Dilemma

Such aversive treatment procedures, if no longer quite "radical," are certainly "intrusive." It is a curious anomaly that, in the United States at a point roughly contemporaneous with the earlier reports from Britain or from North America but often published in British sources, the general tenor of opinion favored the traditional, unfocused, non-invasive, non-intrusive methods of "talking cure" treatment for sex offenders (Annis, 1982; Costell, 1980; Cowden, 1977; Giarreto, 1980; Matek, 1985; Silver, 1976; Smith, 1968; Sterling, 1976). Indeed, in their survey of 22 treatment programs for sex offenders in the U.S. and 12 in Canada, Borzecki & Wormith (1987) observed systematic differences such that the latter were uniformly behaviorist in their orientation. In addition, and not surprisingly a decade after parliamentary repeal of legislation prescribing treatment for criminal sexual psychopaths, programs in Canada, generally based in hospitals, usually required a positive indication of motivation for change as a criterion for admission. In the event, however, it may be that conservative views and practices were to prove prescient in the United States.

Certainly it is the case that substantial public comment was marshaled on both sides of the Atlantic *in opposition* to the treatment modalities proposed by Eysenck, his colleagues and followers, perhaps best expressed artistically by novelist Anthony Burgess in *A Clockwork Orange* (1963), the fictionalized account of the rehabilitation of a criminal psychopath guilty of multiple rape and murder through "Ludovici's technique," essentially a variant of aversive conditioning coupled with psychoactive medication, the effect of which is to create massive physical and psychological stress at the merest thought of the violence that once stimulated and exhilarated. In Burgess' scenario, the forfeiture of "free choice" becomes a major political issue, the terms of which are well enunciated in a monologue by the prison chaplain: "What does God want? Does God want goodness or the *choice* of goodness? Is the man who *chooses the bad* perhaps in some way better than the man who has the good *imposed* on him?" This writer has elsewhere commented on the schizoid posture Western nations have taken in relation to the application of powerful methods of behavior change to criminal offenders, pivoting apparently precisely on the "chaplain's dilemma" (Pallone, 1986, pp. 41–46), even when these methods do *not* require alteration of primitive biochemical processes (as in hormonal suppression) or the "cruel and unusual" mutilation of (voluntary) surgical castration.

In its risk vs. benefit analysis of aversive conditioning as a treatment for criminal sexual psychopathy, the Group for the Advancement of Psychiatry (1977, pp. 896–898) used terms such as "dehumanizing" and "an authoritarian 'treater knows best' posture," questioned whether "as a matter of public policy ... such treatment options should be offered to sex offenders at all," and concluded, with evidence of an unbridled projection that certainly indicates that somebody is obsessed about whether Big Brother is watching:

> aversive treatments for sexual offenses [have] been challenged by both professional and other groups. The fear of "brainwashing" or using treatments for political or social control is always a threat.
> Increasing publicity about the use of various behavioral conditioning techniques for diverse purposes by governments sensitizes the public to potential misuse ... Professionals must keep in mind the potential for abuse of this treatment modality.

Indeed, by the time he published the second edition of *Crime and Personality*, Eysenck (1977, p. 182) felt compelled to answer those critics who had decried the loss of personal freedom on the part of the offenders so treated:

> I have had many requests from prisoners (who had nothing whatever to gain by making such requests) for radical treatment of what they recognized as alien impulses driving them in directions in which they did not want to go; some specifically asked about "brain-washing," conditioning, or even drug treatment. The restructuring of the prisoner's personality is not necessarily going counter to his inner beliefs; there is a war going on within the prisoner, and his better self is asking for help. *That is the ethical basis of the methods here suggested.*

Constraints on Aggressive Treatment

In the United States, in the light of both Federal legislation and judicial decision, the question may be barely moot even in respect of aversive conditioning techniques, let alone such genuinely invasive treatments as surgery, psychosurgery, or hormonal manipulation.

Consider the constraints placed legislatively by the Federal Congress on "experimentation" with human subjects in the biomedical and social science disciplines. Even more pertinently, consider the judicial constraints on treatment modalities for patients in public mental hospitals in the *Wyatt* and *Donaldson* decisions by Mr. Justice Johnson of the Federal District Court in the early 1970s, later upheld by the U.S. Supreme Court [*Note 6*].

These judicial constraints in particular *preclude* the use of aversive treatment of any sort without the "knowing, informed, and voluntary consent" of the patient *and*, in Justice Johnson's words, "the absolute right to terminate ... consent at any time and for any reason." Consider further that it was Mr. Justice Johnson who *also* handed down the decision in *Pugh v. Locke* in 1978, the landmark case that reformed the prisons of Alabama and created the precedent under which the prisons of some 29 other states were to be reformed by order of the Federal courts in the next decade.

The strictures laid down in the *Wyatt* decisions would seem to apply without question to criminal sexual psychopaths confined for treatment in public hospitals. While these strictures have not *yet* been held to apply equally to prisoners as to patients, there are some very special considerations in the case of offenders who have been specifically adjudicated as to be placed in *confinement for purposes of treatment* rather than to be confined punitively, to whom the *Wyatt* strictures would seem to apply without question as well. Only those clinicians and institutional administrators bent on a pathway toward career self-destruction are likely to risk a judicial test, so that, for all practical purposes, *those aggressive methods of treatment that have been demonstrated to be singularly effective in the treatment of compulsive sexual deviance are essentially not employable* on a wide scale in the legislatively-mandated treatment of offenders.

Surely the same strictures apply to the more "heroic" treatment approaches embodied in pharmacotherapy (including chemical or hormonal castration), psychosurgery, and surgical castration. The right of the patient, even the involuntarily committed patient, to refuse the relatively less intrusive therapeutic measure of medication for the treatment of mental illness has now been well established (Brooks, 1986; Rodenhauser, 1984). Even while acknowledging that this right derives from "the basic assumption in our society that all persons have the right to control intrusions on their bodies," distinguished psychiatrist Paid Appelbaum (1988, pp. 413, 415) has underscored the "essential illogic in allowing [involuntarily] committed persons to refuse treatment that would permit their freedom to be restored" [*Note* 7]. That sentiment might undergo several permutations when applied to aggressive treatment modalities for criminally committed sex offenders.

Notes

1. Brecher (1978) examined in some detail the *inpatient* programs at the Adult Diagnostic and Treatment Center, New Jersey; Atascadero State Hospital, California; the Center for the Diagnosis and Treatment of Sexually Dangerous Offenders at Massachusetts Correctional Institution, Bridgewater; Colorado State Reformatory, Buena Vista; Florida State Hospital at Chattahoochie; Metropolitan State Hospital, Norwalk, California; Minnesota Security Hospital, St. Paul; Patton State Hospital, California; South Florida State Hospital, Hollywood; Waupun State Prison, Wisconsin; and Western State Hospital, Fort Steilacoom, Washington. In each of these institutions, group therapy (often focused on "leaderless" or "peer-led" groups in the style of Alcoholics Anonymous) was the principal "standard" treatment modality; in some, provision for individual counseling or psychotherapy, even as adjunctive to "group treatment," was Spartan. Only at Florida State Hospital at Chattahoochie was anything resembling a full range of mental hospital services (occupational therapy, vocational training,

art therapy, religious studies) available to judicially committed criminal sexual psychopaths.

Brecher also described in some detail *outpatient* programs operated by the Center for Behavior Modification, Minneapolis; the Center for Rape Concern, Philadelphia General Hospital; the City of Albuquerque; the Juvenile Probation Department in Santa Clara, California; the Institute for Psychiatry and Law, University of Southern California, Los Angeles; the Phipps Clinic at the Johns Hopkins University School of Medicine, Baltimore; the Department of Psychiatry at the University of Tennessee Center for the Health Sciences at Memphis; the Violence Research Center at Denver General Hospital; and the University of Washington Adolescent Psychiatric Clinic, Seattle. These programs also typically relied on group and individual counseling and psychotherapy as the "standard" treatments, with the exception of the Phipps Clinic, where the distinguished psychologist John Money and his colleagues were experimenting with "reversible chemical castration" through administration of an antiandrogen, and the University of Tennessee, where the distinguished psychiatrist Gene Abel and his colleagues were experimenting with hormonal manipulation in interaction with "aggressive" behavioral counter-conditioning.

The pivot underlying the application of the standard "talking cure" treatment modalities to sex offenders, though unstated, must surely derive from the Freudian canon, which holds in essence that all behavior is rationally controllable once the behaver understands its roots in the unconscious. The canon of behavior therapy and of pharmacotherapy is quite different: behavior is either learned or biochemically controlled or both; when "standard" talking cures prove ineffective, the *humane* choice for the person in distress is to seek a more "aggressive" treatment.

2. The pivotal issue in assessment of successful treatment of the criminal sexual psychopath is the selection of the *criterion behaviors* against which to gauge success or failure (Davies, 1979; Rezmovic, 1979). From the mental health perspective, the appropriate "criterion behaviors" are those that reflect disordered, inappropriate, or developmentally-arrested mental or emotional processes; from the criminal justice perspective the appropriate "criterion behaviors" are those that result in re-arrest and re-conviction. Throughout the arena encompassed by offender rehabilitation, it is not uncommon that psychologically disordered behavior patterns are indeed successfully treated *but that* successful treatment either does not reduce the probability of criminal recidivism or indeed actually *accelerates* that probability. The common experience of the aftermath of the introduction of "assertiveness training" into offender rehabilitation regimens can serve to illustrate. It is a commonplace that many offenders seem to lack the interpersonal skills activated in self-assertion, perhaps attributable to low levels of self-esteem, which are thought to be lifelong and to be the product of such factors as race, low socioeconomic status in the family of origin, poor academic adjustment in childhood and adolescence, and the like. From such considerations, it should follow that persons low in self-assertive skill are likely to "follow the leader" so as to gain peer acceptance; and to this set of factors is to be attributed involvement (at least, as an accomplice rather than as a principal) in many types of criminal activity.

Mental health clinicians have developed a wide array of "treatment" techniques that yield dependably an increase in self-assertion skills. It would seem to follow as the night the day that application of these techniques to convicted and incarcerated offenders should yield healthier personalities capable of withstanding "peer pressure" to engage in criminal activity. Accordingly, self-assertion training was introduced into prison settings, with the typical result that, at the end of such training, prisoners indeed scored substantially higher on paper-and-pencil as well as behavioral measures of self-assertive capacity; thus, from the perspective of mental health clinicians, such training could justifiably be regarded as successful. *But such increases in self-assertive capacity were abo behaviorally reflected in increases in assaultive behavior against prison guards.* From the criminal justice perspective, it is substantially easier to manage correctional institutions peopled by non-assertive types, so that a "throw the shrinks and other rascals out" attitude following *successful* treatment is entirely understandable (Beidelman, 1981; Marshall, Keltner & Marshall, 1981).

3. Quinsey's (1983) judgment concerning the superiority of behavior therapy to other forms of psychological treatment when applied to criminally deviant sexuality is precisely congruent with a strong body of research evidence that suggests behavior therapy's greater efficacy when applied to a panoply of emotional and psychological disorders quite independent of either sexuality or criminality (Bergin & Lambert, 1978; Eysenck, 1966; Rachman & Wilson, 1980; Rimland, 1966).

4. Groth, Longo & McFadin (1982) would doubtless quarrel with utilization of subsequent arrest and conviction data as criterion measures for effectiveness of treatment. In a study of some 140 convicted sexual psychopaths, they found that "the majority of the offenders admitted to having committed two to five times as many sex crimes [as those for which they have been] apprehended ... For this reason, recidivism, as judged by re-arrests, is not a dependable measure of rehabilitation of the sexual offender." In their comprehensive review of studies of recidivism among sex offenders, whether treated or not, Furby, Weinrott & Blackshaw (1989) reach a roughly congruent conclusion. When applied to Dix's analysis, however, this argument would veer in an unexpected direction; that is, one should expect the recidivism rate among *treated* offenders to be higher than that reported, but the same argument might not hold among punitively *incarcerated* and *untreated* offenders. In contrast, however, in a study of the subsequent convictions of exhibitionists, Berah & Myers (1983) found no characteristic progression either to more serious sex crimes nor to more serious crimes of violence.

5. Similarly, Schoenthaler (1983) has reported a 62% decrease in assaultive behavior among convicted and incarcerated rapists (along with equally impressive reductions among inmates convicted of other offenses) by the simple manipulation of the level of intake of refined sugar.

6. A relatively large proportion of the precedents cited by Mr. Justice Johnson in the *Wyatt* decisions involved cases brought by, or on behalf of, persons who had been convicted and confined for treatment under the terms of sex offender legislation in the several states. In the analysis of the *Wyatt* decisions provided by Fremouw (1976), pivotal precedents include *Miller v. Overholser*, 1953, in which the court ordered that treatment be provided to an offender "involuntarily confined under a remedial sexual psychopath statute" in the District of Columbia; *People v. Levy*, 1957, concerning an offender sentenced to be confined for treatment in California as a "sexual psychopath" with no upper limit specified; and *In re Maddox*, 1958, in which the court ruled that treatment, rather than custodial confinement, must be accorded to an offender convicted under Michigan's criminal sexual psychopath laws. The *Wyatt* decisions (*Wyatt v. Stickney, Wyatt v. Alderholt, Wyatt v. Hardin*) and those in attendant cases (*Donaldson v. O'Connor, O'Connor v. Donaldson*) through the level of the Supreme Court are reproduced in their entirety by Golann & Fremouw (1976). Mr. Justice Johnson's decision in Pugh v. Locke is reproduced in 406 *Federal Supplement* 318, 1976, pp. 332–337.

7. In a decision announced on February 27, 1990 (*Washington v. Harper*, 88–599), the scope of which is really quite limited, the U.S. Supreme Court opened a "window" on the matter of *involuntary* administration of psychotropic medication to prisoners. The specific case concerned the acceptability under the Constitution of the procedures used in the state of Washington to determine whether psychoactive

medication should be administered to an inmate against his or her will. Those procedures require the decision of a review board composed of a prison psychiatrist, a prison psychologist, and a correctional administrator to overrule the inmate's declination; the inmate has the right to be represented by an advisor but not by an attorney. The key phrases in the Supreme Court's decision hold that the state is Constitutionally permitted (with emphases added) "to treat a prison inmate who has a serious mental illness with antipsychotic drugs against his will, *if the inmate is dangerous to himself or others* and the treatment is in the inmate's medical interest."

Clearly, it is the "clear and imminent danger" test (reviewed in Chapter 4) that has been applied by the Court in its reasoning, so that the scope of the decision appears limited to those situations in which an inmate presents an imminent threat of *violence* within the correctional setting. That is a situation at some considerable conceptual and operational distance from the involuntary administration of medication to treat a disorder *on account of which* an inmate has become an inmate but which cannot reasonably be linked to the prospect of suicide or assault while in custody—for example, in the case of focused pedophiles confined in an institution for adults. Even though the scope of *Washington v. Harper* would seem to preclude such aggressive pharmacotherapy as chemical castration in the rehabilitative treatment of sex offenders, the window has been opened for future litigation—perhaps, indeed, brought by sex offenders as *plaintiffs* who would prefer chemical castration (followed by release) over continued confinement for nonpharmacotherapeutic treatment.

It is a matter of some interest that the American Psychiatric Association filed an *amicus* brief favoring the position of the state, while the American Psychological Association filed its *amicus* brief on the side of the inmate. The position of the American Psychological Association is particularly curious at a time when a vocal segment of its membership had raised a clamor demanding that psychologists be granted the right to prescribe psychoactive medication in their own clinical practices.

6 Exits
Differential Criteria and Pathways
for Release

How the person incarcerated as a felony sex offender under the jurisdiction of the correctional authority achieves release from confinement differs markedly, both in respect of the criteria to be satisfied and the pathways to be negotiated, from how the criminal sexual psychopath sentenced to confinement "for purposes of treatment" under the jurisdiction *either* of the mental health authority or the correctional authority is released.

Release from Confinement as a Prisoner

Barring only a gubernatorial grant of clemency, to be released from punitive confinement in prison under the jurisdiction of the correctional authority in any state one must either serve the full term of his or her sentence or achieve parole. In most jurisdictions, when the sentence is *determinate*, with both upper and lower limits specified by the sentencing judge, parole is granted in consequence of some combination of time served (usually a proportion in the range of 25% to 33% of the *lower* limit of the sentence judicially imposed) and the record of the inmate's behavior within the institution, with implicit or explicit consideration of the severity of the offense(s)-of-record in connection with the instant sentence and of the prospective parolee's prior criminal history [*Note* 1].

Behavior within the institution includes both the record of disciplinary infractions, satisfactory completion of work assignmerits, and whether the inmate took advantage of whatever additional programs (e.g., educational or vocational training, participation in Alcoholics Anonymous and the like, even counseling if offered) were made available, but *without* particular effort to determine in any measurable way whether the prisoner derived "benefit" from such additional activity or whether such participation yielded demonstrable "effect" in reducing the prospect of future criminal behavior.

When the sentence is *indeterminate*, with only the upper limit specified by the sentencing judge, by design little attention is paid to proportion of time served, but the other variables remain relatively constant. In either case, implicitly or by policy or design, *the prisoner has available to him or her a relatively explicit set of criteria whereby he or she can judge the probability of his* or her release on parole [*Note* 2]. There will ensue consideration by the paroling authority, which may include a personal interview with the inmate; that interview may tangentially, and generally only superficially, touch upon such issues as "benefit" or "demonstrable effect" in reducing future dangerousness.

Release from Confinement as a Mental Patient

To be released from *voluntary* or *civil* commitment as a patient in a public mental hospital customarily requires no more than the decision of the facility's superintendent, itself generally predicated on the recommendation of the mental health clinicians principally responsible for providing treatment; in all cases, *voluntary* patients retain the right to terminate treatment "against medical advice" at any time and for any reason.

In some states, to be released from a *criminal* commitment to a psychiatric hospital similarly requires no more than the decision of the superintendent. In other states, release requires review by a board or committee drawn from the institution and/or from the mental health community [*Note* 3]; and, in yet others, such release may occur only upon order of the court that issued the commitment order. In most cases, *the patient himself or herself has little in the way of explicit, objective criteria whereby he or she can estimate the probability of release and his or her progress leading thereto*, though the criminally committed patient retains the right to challenge at law professional recommendations for continued hospitalization [*Note* 4].

The patient who has been criminally committed as a result of an insanity acquittal has, in effect, admitted that he or she behaved contrary to the provisions of law; but the insanity acquittal has in effect exculpated him or her from criminal responsibility. There is no particular reason why a person accused of a "property" offense might not invoke an insanity defense, arguing for example that he or she suffers from a deep psychosis that expresses itself in kleptomania; in actual practice, however, an insanity defense is rarely invoked except in crimes that involve life-threatening behavior: homicide, rape, atrocious assault, and, in jurisdictions that still prosecute for the offense, attempted suicide.

Especially in a time of understaffed and underfunded public facilities, to merit commitment to psychiatric hospitalization following insanity acquittal in practice virtually requires that the behavior to which the patient has implicitly admitted constitute life-threatening or otherwise seriously dangerous behavior; the hypothetical kleptomaniac who succeeded at an insanity defense is more likely to be sentenced to probation, likely with outpatient mental health treatment as a condition.

To that extent, in the judgment of the American Psychiatric Association in its Statement on the Insanity Defense (1984, pp. 20–21), "the 'dangerousness' of insanity acquitees who have perpetrated violence has already been demonstrated. Their future dangerousness need not be inferred; it may be assumed." The sentiment hardly accords with the Association's (1974) stern warnings on the assessment of future violence. Nevertheless, *future dangerousness* or, at least, the judgment that the criminally committed patient is *no longer dangerous* to others or to himself or herself presumably represents the pivotal *criterion* governing release of those criminally committed to psychiatric hospitalization [*Note* 5].

Release from Confinement for Treatment

Under the relevant legislation, the criminal sexual psychopath who is confined for treatment almost invariably is accorded an "indeterminate" sentence (i.e., one with only an upper limit specified), with release prior to termination of that sentence pivoting on the *clinical* judgment that he or she has been "treated" so successfully that he or she no longer suffers from criminal sexual psychopathy and thus no longer represents a threat to the social order. In some jurisdictions, the criminal sexual psychopath is accorded an *indefinite* sentence, so that not even an upper limit is judicially imposed; in such cases, release is entirely contingent on clinical judgment and has no relationship whatever to the passage of time.

In those states where treatment is provided under the jurisdiction of the health authority, the pathway governing release from criminal commitment will prevail. That pathway will surely include professional mental health assessment of the offender's progress in treatment, activating a set of variables substantially beyond the control of the individual thus confined.

In some states where treatment is under the jurisdiction of the correctional authority, an uninflected parole pathway will be available. But in yet other states where treatment is under the jurisdiction of the correctional authority, a crossover pathway has also been legislatively mandated, whereby a recommendation for release on parole as a result of progress in treatment is to be *independently* validated by a "dangerousness review board." Usually composed of mental health and social service professionals not associated with the facility in which treatment is provided, so as to obviate self-validation of the judgments of the staff of that facility, the board is generally required to render its independent judgment of the effects of treatment *before* an application for parole will be considered by the paroling authority.

That crossover pathway hinges on these considerations: (*1*) That, if an offender is confined largely as the result of "clinical judgment," he or she should be released only when clinical judgment as to the likelihood of future criminal sexual behavior is satisfied, (*2*) that such clinical judgment on the part of the mental health professionals responsible for treatment of the offender should independently withstand the scrutiny of the mental health community represented by members of a pre-parole review board implicitly or explicitly charged with estimating future dangerousness, *and* (*3*) that the clinical judgments of the treaters and the reviewers should be persuasive as well to those public officers charged with the granting of parole in all criminal cases (Roberts & Pacht, 1965), whether or not sexual in character.

Whether made by mental health professionals in the institution charged with providing treatment *or* by members of clinical review boards at subsequent stages, *clinical judgments* that the criminal sexual psychopath no longer suffers from this condition and that he or she thus no longer presents a threat to society would seem to require clear conceptualizations and correlated empirical referents concerning both sexual psychopathy and future dangerousness. But, as Chapter 2 has suggested, there is not only no "clear conceptualization" of criminal sexual psychopathy in the mental health community but indeed strong support for the elimination of this legislatively created "diagnostic category." One should not be surprised, therefore, that there obtains no standard litany of empirical referents correlated therewith, as Chapter 4 has indicated. Further, not only does there not obtain a clear set of conceptual and empirical referents for the prediction of prospective dangerousness, but both the American Psychiatric and American Psychological Association have taken strong official positions counter to predictions of future violence. These circumstances appear to congeal into a clinical quandary of rather massive proportions.

Assessing the Effectiveness of Treatment

The criminal sex offender *not* sentenced for treatment but instead confined for punishment would appear to be in a position to exercise far greater control over his or her fate than an "otherwise similar" offender confined for treatment. Felony offenders who have been punitively incarcerated can control relatively more readily the extent to which their behavior constitutes a problem in discipline control to custodial personnel, whether they report faithfully to a work assignment, whether they avoid physical conflict with other inmates, and the like. But the offender confined for treatment exercises relatively less control over his or her progress in therapy, the skill and acuity of treating personnel, or even the efficacy of the methods of treatment that can be applied under the constraints of judicial precedent and institutional policy.

To some very major extent, when the members of a clinical pre-parole board under the correctional authority or a clinical "dangerousness review board" under the mental health authority judge readiness for release on the part of a criminal sexual psychopath, they judge not merely how energetically the offender has participated in whatever "treatment" program has been made available to him or her, *but also the efficacy of the methods of treatment and the clinical skill of the treating agents* [Note 6]. There is opportunity aplenty for challenges to a release process that pivots on the assessment of the efficacy of the treatment accorded to an individual offender, under terms of that which can be accorded within judicially- and legislatively-constrained institutional policies, and appropriately delivered in consequence of the level of knowledge and skill represented among institutional staff.

A Prospective Right to Effective Treatment?

In upholding the decisions of Mr. Justice Johnson in the *Wyatt* and *Donaldson* cases, the U.S. Supreme Court has declared that patients in mental hospitals have an absolute right to treatment and that to confine patients in the absence of treatment in effect constitutes involuntary imprisonment, in violation of Constitutional guarantees against deprivation of liberty without due process (Golann & Fremouw, 1978, pp. 129–185). In his *Pugh v. Locke* decision of 1976, also upheld by the Supreme Court, Mr. Justice Johnson established the right of prisoners not merely to sanitary and "humane" living conditions but also to "meaningful programs" [*Note* 7]. While the court has shown some disposition to pronounce upon what constitutes "inappropriate" treatment, it has not yet addressed the question of whether the patient or the prisoner has a right to *effective* treatment.

In New Jersey, the "due process" issue was raised in suits brought by an offender confined under terms of the state's criminal sexual psychopath legislation who simply refused to participate in the treatment program accorded him, in the first instance against the present writer as chairperson of the state's pre-parole review board and against the chief psychologist of Rahway State Prison and in the second instance against the writer, the governor of the state, and the Federal District judge who ruled unfavorably in the first case [*Note* 8]. What was at issue in these cases was indeed the "right to treatment," but essentially in reverse fashion, for the matter hinged on the *refusal* of plaintiff to participate in the therapeutic program offered to him within the treatment facility.

The basic formulation followed these lines:

- *You have confined me for treatment. I am not being treated, because what you have to offer is not acceptable to me. You have re-assigned me to a general prison routine. Therefore, you are not treating me, as you are required to do. Since I am confined for treatment and am not being treated, let me go.*

The court chose not to intrude into what it continues to regard as the realm of professional judgment as to what constitutes "treatment" under the law, nor to essay the thornier question of what constitutes "appropriate" treatment for a particular inmate or patient. In those decisions, the court was in consonance with decisions in other jurisdictions from the early 1950s onward (Golann & Fremouw, 1976, pp. 8–9). In *Millard v. Cameron*, for example, the Federal District Court for the District of Columbia in 1966 declared that it lacked competence to determine what constitutes "treatment" for a criminal sexual psychopath. Thus, it ordered the plaintiff, who had a long history of exhibitionism and who had been incarcerated at St. Elizabeth's Hospital in Washington for several years as a criminal sexual psychopath, in a program of "treatment" that consisted of a work assignment to mop the floors of his ward, to be remanded for a continuation of what the court could not, or would not, decide constituted "treatment," let alone "appropriate" or "effective" treatment. Had Millard been confined as a felony offender, the sanction for the instant offense would have been 90 days in Lorton Reformatory.

On the basis of the *Wyatt, Donaldson*, and *Pugh* decisions, and within a context in which the very notion of criminal sexual psychopathy has little support among mental health professionals, one may confidently expect more carefully framed challenges in the future. Those challenges may well pivot on *equal access to prospectively effective treatment*, in some formulation similar to this:

- *You have judicially confined me, not for punishment, but for treatment. It is your obligation to treat me effectively, since I can't be released from confinement unless I am judged to have been treated successfully. It is therefore your obligation to treat me effectively—but within the legislative and judicial strictures laid down judicially governing mental health treatment of involuntary patients. Treat me effectively or let me go. That you have not, in your collective wisdom, yet discovered effective treatment methods for people like me that meet those strictures is your problem, not mine. To continue to confine me while you apply traditional treatment methods that have limited chance of success constitutes punishment and violates the clear intent of the law.*

And it is at that point that the amalgam of clinical quandaries turn about to become a legislative morass [*Note 9*].

Notes

1. Without question, the most significant research on how parole decisions are actually made in practice, in comparison to and in contrast with legislatively-mandated or otherwise explicitly stated criteria, has been reported by Gottfredson and his colleagues in a carefully executed series of investigations over nearly two decades (Gottfredson & Ballard, 1966; Gottfredson, Wilkins & Hoffman, 1978; Gottfredson, Cosgrove, Wilkins, Wallerstein & Rauh, 1978; Gottfredson & Gottfredson, 1980). On the basis of this research, an explicit set of guidelines in the parole decision process was promulgated throughout the Federal prison system, emphasizing severity of offense-of-record for the present sentence and prior criminal history as the governing variables, and several state systems adopted similar approaches. When a parole recommendation is denied, the paroling authority operating under such a system is required to state its reasons in writing; in application, the "guidelines system" permits the inmate to estimate the point at which it becomes rational for him or her to expect favorable consideration for parole.
2. As Gottfredson & Gottfredson (1980, pp. 283–284) suggest, parole is regarded as a *privilege* rather than as a "right." Nonetheless, under color of Constitutional guarantees of due process, the case can be made that all inmates should have "equal access" to the "privilege" of parole. Such considerations appeared to loom large in the decision of paroling authorities to adopt, and in some cases to publish, explicit parole decision guidelines.

3. In its Statement on the Insanity Defense, the American Psychiatric Association (1984, pp. 22–23) stipulated that "The American Psychiatric Association believes that the decision to release an insanity acquitee should not be made solely by psychiatrists or *solely* on the basis of psychiatric testimony about the patient's mental condition or predictions of future dangerousness." The Association thus recommends that "Confinement and release decisions should be made by a board constituted to include psychiatrists and other professionals representing the criminal justice system, akin to a parole board" and that "The board having jurisdiction over released insanity acquitees should have clear authority to reconfine."

   Reinehr, Dudley & White (1985) studied the operation of "dangerousness review boards" composed in this fashion and empowered in Texas to make determinations concerning the prospective dangerousness of psychiatric patients prior to release both before and after expansion of the membership of such boards from psychiatrists exclusively to include social workers, psychologists, and attorneys as well, finding that the multidisciplinary boards certified *fewer* patients as not dangerous.

4. Forensic psychiatrists Seymour Halleck (1987, pp. 96–100) and Robert Simon (1987, pp. 339–358) discuss the matter of professional liability for "negligent release" when an accused offender found not guilty by reason of insanity commits a subsequent crime after release from mandatory treatment and when such release proceeds *without* judicial approbation. But it is not self-evident that *judicial* decisions to release an offender from criminal commitment *on the basis of professional recommendations* would exculpate the professionals who made the pivotal recommendations should future violence ensue.

   From the perspective of the mental health professional, the issue engages the question of the state of the art concerning the prediction of future dangerousness (reviewed in Chapter 4). From the perspective of the patient, the key issue is the rectitude of confining a person who has *not* been found guilty of a criminal act (*precisely because* the insanity plea has been successful) *beyond* the point at which those responsible for the treatment of his or her mental disorder believe he or she is either "cured" or sufficiently improved to return to the community. Is it ethically, and under the Fourteenth Amendment constitutionally, permissible to confine such an accused offender for a period greater than that for which a putatively "otherwise similar" mentally ill person who has not been accused of crime is customarily confined? And if, in the judgment of the mental health professionals, the accused offender found not guilty by reason of insanity has improved sufficiently to warrant release in the judgment of those responsible for his or her treatment, is it not likely that continued confinement violates the mental patient's right to treatment established in a series of U.S. Supreme Court decisions?

5. After lamenting that "the nature of in-hospital psychiatric intervention has changed over the last decade" so that "greater emphasis is now placed on psychopharmacological management of the hospitalized person" and warning that "such treatment, while clearly helpful in reducing the overt signs and symptoms of mental illness, does not necessarily mean that 'cure' has been achieved, nor that a patient's 'nondangerousness' is assured," the American Psychiatric Association's Statement on the Insanity Defense (1984, p. 21) rather pontifically declaims: "The American Psychiatric Association is therefore quite skeptical about procedures now implemented in many states requiring periodic decisionmaking by mental health professionals (or by others) concerning a requirement that insanity acquittees who have committed previous violent offenses be repetitively adjudicated as 'dangerous,' thereby provoking their release once future dangerousness cannot be clearly demonstrated in accord with the standard of proof required."

6. Though it has been reasonably well established that such "criminological" indices as offense history predict with some accuracy recidivism across the range of offenders

of all sorts, Hall & Proctor (1987) found that such is not the case among sex offenders. Using sophisticated statistical techniques, these investigators reported that the magnitude of the relationships observed between criminological indices and recidivism "does not warrant the sole use of criminological variables for decisions regarding individual sex offenders." Such data might support an inference that clinical judgment about treatment progress is indeed called for in such cases, if only there were any reason to believe that clinical judgment was in any way superior to actuarial prediction; alternately, the data might be interpreted to mean that sex offenders are less predictable than other offenders, even actuarially.

7. Golann & Fremouw (1976) review in detail the series of cases involving the rights of mental patients, including those confined by judicial action following prosecution for criminal behavior. Among the work's many interesting features are "eyewitness" accounts by Stonewall B. Stickney, Alabama's commissioner of mental health and therefore the chief executive officer for the state's public psychiatric hospitals during the prosecution of the landmark cases that established, at the level of the U.S. Supreme Court, the rights of mental patients. Other fascinating eyewitness accounts of his personal role in shaping and prosecuting the landmark case (*Pugh v. Locke*, 406 Federal Supplement 318, 1976) that, also at the Supreme Court level, established the rights of prisoners to "meaningful programs" are provided by distinguished psychologist Raymond Fowler (1976,1988).

8. The cases in question are *Artway v. Pallone & Rotgers* and *Artway v. Pallone, [Gov. Brendan] Byrne, [Federal District Judge Frederick] Stern, et al.*, adjudicated in the Federal district court for the First District of New Jersey in 1979–80 in decisions upheld by the U.S. Court of Appeals for the Third Circuit (80–1980). Similar issues related to a prisoner's right to refuse treatment are discussed by Sherlock (1984) and Veneziano (1986).

On November 29, 1989, a suit was filed in Federal District Court, under color of the Fourteenth Amendment's guarantees against undue restriction of liberty, on behalf of the Inmate Resident Committee of the Adult Diagnostic and Treatment Center, the unit in the New Jersey Department of Corrections charged with executing the legislative mandate of providing treatment for adjudicated criminal sexual psychopaths. The suit comes very close to raising the issue of a right to *effective* treatment by asserting, *inter alia*, that "Inmates committed to the custody and care of the New Jersey Department of Corrections are entitled to receive reasonable medical care ... and this includes the right to psychiatric or psychological as well as physical care"; that "Offenders sentenced to ... a program of 'specialized treatment' are entitled to receive rehabilitative therapy"; that there is no comprehensive program of specialized treatment "as mandated by law ... for each individual offender, including coordinating therapy, educational, vocational, recreational, and work activities" so as to thus constitute a focused rehabilitative regimen; and (in an allegation that unwittingly raises a variety of *Pugh v. Locke* issues) that "The lack of adequate staff, facility, and/or funds is not a sufficient excuse to deny offenders sentenced to the ADTC rehabilitative therapy as required by their sentences." Named as defendants in the suit are the Governor of the state, the Commissioner of Corrections, the superintendent of the institution, the chairperson of the state's parole board, and the present writer in his capacity as chairperson of the Special Classification Review Board for Sex Offenders, along with a variety of others concerned with the operation of the institution and/or the process of release therefrom. Significantly, the suit does not seek relief in the form of release from confinement for treatment—but instead *asks the courts to compel compliance with the law so as to insure relevant, focused, and specific* treatment. As the present manuscript was completed, the suit had only just begun its slow progress through the court system.

9. Indeed, with the issuance of a massive 3,300–page, four-volume compendium of "standard" treatment techniques for mental disorders of all sorts by the American Psychiatric Press, the publishing arm of the American Psychiatric Association (Karasu et al., 1989), one expects the decade of the 1990s to be characterized by extraordinary litigation for negligent malpractice directed against mental health professionals who have *not* applied in individual cases those treatment techniques approbated by the APA Task Force responsible for the compendium. Even though the document specifically does not carry the formal endorsement of APA, and despite the strong demurrers among non-psychiatrist mental health professionals (principally because of its heavy reliance on pharmacotherapy) and even among some members of the psychiatric community, the compendium is certain to be interpreted at law as the repository of the collective wisdom of the professional group dominant in the treatment of mental illness. When applied to the criminal sexual psychopath, the argument might be made: *If the treatment you have provided me does not conform to the "standard" treatment for whatever disorder(s) you think I have—as indicated in the compendium that represents the best available current thinking in the psychiatric community—you have deprived me of liberty without sufficient cause. Such deprivation seems, prima facie, to violate Fourteenth Amendment guarantees; and such deprivation willfully can be construed not merely as negligent practice with civil consequences for you, but perhaps even as criminally conspiratorial to deprive me of my rights under the Constitution.* The decade ahead augurs lively for judicial intervention in the legislatively-mandated treatment of criminal sexual psychopaths.

7 Reprise
The Clinical Quandaries Revisited

This volume has essayed to identify the clinical quandaries generated by legislation that prescribes differential sanctioning for persons who commit sex crimes incidentally to other felonies and those who are presumably driven by psychosexual pathology.

Such legislation calls upon the mental health professions, during the process of evaluation that eventuates in recommendations to the court concerning disposition, to make distinctions for which there is little sound scientific support. To the extent that psychosexual pathology itself constitutes a mental disorder within the current lexicon that guides the mental health professions, distinguished forensic psychiatrist Seymour Halleck (1987) can hardly be gainsaid when he asserts that any offender found guilty of a sex crime can be "automatically" categorized as *mentally disordered*, from which it seems to follow that *either all or none* should be accorded the "differential" sanction of legislatively-mandated treatment.

Even though treatment programs designed to implement the legislative mandate typically rely on rather tame forms of the "talking cure," a variety of specific treatment modalities, generally aggregated under the descriptor *aversive behavior therapy* and sometimes including biochemical manipulation of sensitivity to sexual stimuli, have convincingly demonstrated their effectiveness when applied to sex offenders on both sides of the Atlantic. Yet judicial constraints seem to preclude their use on a wide scale. Thus, legislation that requires that mentally disordered sex offenders be confined for treatment implicitly mandates, within the context of those constraints, confinement for *less than optimally effective* treatment. To the extent that release from such confinement is predicated upon satisfactory progress in treatment and to the extent that treatment modalities that are, or can be, provided are thus constrained, the access of the offender so sanctioned to *prospectively effective* treatment appears to the same extent compromised.

Moreover, the process of release from confinement for treatment as a criminal sexual psychopath—in some sharp contrast to the process of release from confinement for punishment as a felony sex offender—requires a *positive* recommendation on the part of mental health clinicians responsible for providing treatment that the person in question is no longer dangerous. Yet the official position of both the American Psychiatric Association and the American Psychological Association urges that the state of the art in such prediction is so flawed that the process must be abandoned. In some states, where the additional layer of review by a panel of mental health specialists drawn from the community to validate or gainsay an institutional recommendation is also legislatively mandated, this problem is geometrically compounded.

An Epilogue in First Person

Were one to abandon the role of presumably detached scientific observer assumed to compose a more-or-less scholarly tome in order to speculate personally on the past, present, and future of the legislatively-mandated mental health treatment of criminal sexual deviance, the resulting ruminations might run like this:

Through its legislatures, society has called upon me and others like me to execute its injunctions. For whatever set of reasons, likely by now obscured beyond recognition, you, members of the legislatures, enacted a series of laws that call upon us to do that which is virtually impossible. You have asked us, in the first instance, to sort rapists, child molesters, those given to bestiality, and a variety of other unsavory types into two categories; and indeed to do so by means of those standard sorting, or measuring, devices that meet legal standards for "customary practice" in our professions.

But the leading minds in our professions really seem to be telling us that the effort to accomplish that sorting task is doomed from the outset, since one of the categories into which you wish us to sort exists in any real sense only in your minds.

That is not to say, however, that we can't detect aberrant sexuality; and it doesn't particularly matter to us whether the process of detection is undertaken pursuant to legislation and an order of the court or not.

We can detect aberrant sexuality by means of measures of psycho-physiologic reactivity to aberrant sexual stimuli, with a degree of certitude that substantially surpasses that associated with a battery of psychological tests and clinical interviews. But those psychophysiologic measures require expensive laboratory equipment and are labor-intensive in their application; be prepared, when next you see the asking budgets for the institutions to which you have assigned the task of detection, to meet the additional costs that will be engendered. And, since the use of these psychophysiologic measures has not yet become "customary practice" in our professions, both you and we had better be prepared for all sorts of legal challenges from defense counsel. Of course, if you want a personal guess, I'll wager that the widespread application of such relevant, scientifically sound measures will render your "felony sex offender" category virtually an empty set.

Do not misunderstand; I do not propose to eliminate the "standard and customary" psychometric instruments from the evaluative process. But what I do propose is that they be used to detect facitiousness or dissembling and to assess amenability to, and motivation for, undergoing those forms of treatment for aberrant sexuality that are focused, specific, relevant, and aggressive.

In the second instance, you call upon us to provide treatment for aberrant sexuality; yet other societal forces, notably the U.S. Congress and the courts, constrain us from using those methods of treatment that have been demonstrated scientifically as especially potent—unless the offender who is to be treated is able to provide "knowing, informed, and voluntary consent." Otherwise, the courts have said, aversive treatment would constitute punishment. And you, members of the legislatures, have decided that criminal sexual psychopaths shouldn't be punished. We leave that legal quandary to you. For my own part, I wouldn't quibble about the distinction between "punishment" and "treatment"; in fact, I think we might have an interesting discussion about whether confinement for treatment in a situation that constrains treatment modalities to the largely unfocused, non-specific, and/or the inappropriate and irrelevant itself might not be construed as punitive—and not only, for that matter, for the treatee.

But let's also be clear about the economics of the situation. The sort of treatment I'm talking about is costly and labor-intensive. In contrast to a single clinician, say, working with six to ten inmates in a group therapy situation, that treatment which is focused, specific, appropriate, and relevant would require a treatment team heavily laden with health service professionals. To treat a single offender, we'd need a psychiatrist or a psychologist (fully trained and credentialed at the doctoral level, not merely one with a master's degree who's willing to work for the substandard salaries accorded to institutional personnel); a physician; perhaps an anesthetist; and a nurse; plus security personnel. Further, the team could operate efficiently only in a hospital, not in a prison facility.

For most offenders, the treatment can well progress without the introduction of psychoactive medication intended to remedy whatever neurochemical or neuroanatomical deficits or anomalies may underlay abnormal psychophysiological reactivity to sexual stimuli. That should please those who distrust contemporary psychiatry's reliance on medication as a means of behavior control, fearing that those so medicated will be able to "choose" neither the good nor the evil. Let's just suppress any thoughts we might have about those who can't "choose" to avoid victimization by people who "choose" the evil. And we'll similarly suppress any Third Reich-like thoughts about castration, whether chemical or surgical, voluntary or involuntary.

But we've got to be clear that the treatment team I've described would be spending weeks on end, perhaps months, with a single offender. What we can deliver to you at the end of that time will be a person who has been deconditioned from responding to aberrant stimuli; and we will be in a position to affirm, barring only willful reconditioning on his or her part or "accidental" reconditioning through some unimaginable confluence of contingencies, that he or she is unlikely in the immediate future to behave in sexually criminal ways. That seems to me a better basis for a release decision than any of the systems now in place. We can, of course, hedge our bets if you allow us to require lifelong re-certification of non-responsiveness to such stimuli, along with a mandate for re-admission to treatment facilities for "booster" treatment when that appears necessary. I'm not sure what you would say either to the American Civil Liberties Union or to the High Justices about all that, however.

Understand quite clearly that we can't promise anything like non-recidivism, even when we certify that the successfully treated offender is ready for release; but our powers of prognostication, or guessing in plainer language, should be considerably enhanced if we have used aggressive means to extirpate deviant reactivity to aberrant sexual stimuli—which is, more or less, the starting point for this particular merry-go-round—and base a treater's recommendation for release on publically verifiable scientific evidence that such deviant reactivity no longer occurs.

And there is another, and quite massive, problem. If you enable such a program of treatment legislatively and your judicial colleagues similarly permit, we could expect to successfully treat and to propose to release as relatively safe the majority of offenders in far less time than the years now spent in confinement, whether for treatment or for punishment. Your cost accountants will have to tell you whether, in the long haul, you'll save or spend money if you substitute a hospital-based, labor-intensive, but relatively shorter-term, program for one that is corrections-based, non-labor-intensive, but relatively longer-term. But both of us know quite well that you will pay a heavy political price for such a substitution; and all we would need is a single unpredicted case of recidivism to energize into a common cause both the civil libertarians and the women's liberationists.

That price, you may well decide, is simply too great; nor could anyone who lives near the world of realpolitik disagree. Must you be content, then, to retain the present unsatisfactory state of affairs?

Not if you choose a middle course, as our brothers to the North have done in Canada. You could well render treatment such as has been described an option *for those offenders whom we certify to you are appropriate and well motivated candidates, with punishment as the standard sanction for criminal sexual behavior. Still, you must be prepared to see those offenders who opt for treatment and who are treated successfully achieve release over the relatively shorter term. That may be an appropriate price for a society that both conceives itself as humane and caring (else you would not have enacted those laws that create artificially distinct categories in the first place), also prides itself on scientific and technological advances, and, not incidentally, harbors some sentimental notions about redemption as well.*

So far, we've not talked about the issue of prevention at all. The body of knowledge in the neurosciences has, until now, only been able to post-dict those brain-behavior anomalies that distinguish certain sexual deviancies. But I am confident that, very possibly within the next decade, the explosion of knowledge in the neurosciences will enable us to predict with reasonable accuracy those who, on the basis of brain-behavior anomalies alone, are at high risk for violent criminal sexual deviancy. Those who remain enamored of such notions as "preventive detention" and other such social control mechanisms as render totalitarian societies more readily manageable than libertarian democracies might greet such a prospect with glee, for it would provide a scientific-looking basis to "lock'em up before they have a chance to do anything." Lombroso would be delighted, but the price is surely too high to contemplate.

On the other hand, that state of knowledge may allow us to enumerate a scientifically grounded litany of "risk factors" that might become the basis for educative efforts, particularly among those citizens whose neural anomalies have come to medical attention. To inform an individual that he or she is at risk for criminal offending sexually at a certain degree of probability is analogous to public health efforts to inform an individual that he or she is at risk to contract a physical disease of one sort or another; it is also an invitation to that individual to undertake those compensatory or remedial steps that are likely to defeat the prediction. We might even want to discuss whether, without knowledge that he or she is at risk, there can be genuine "choice" for anyone.

And you will scarcely quibble that it is only by providing the opportunity for an informed choice that a caring, libertarian democracy can reasonably hope to resolve its Chaplain's Dilemma.

Counterpoint at about 160 Degrees

There are surely those who will sputter at the last sentence, replete with its intentional heart-tug, no less than at the implicit agenda it is intended to recapitulate. They will be persuaded that executing such an agenda constitutes an awful lot of trouble; and they will be tempted to abandon treatment as a sanctioning alternative altogether, opting squarely for the single and universal sanction of punishment instead. Repeal the laws, they will argue, rather than revise them so as to render treatment voluntary, Canada-style, for only those sex offenders some bunch of self-serving shrinks claim they can "certify" as representing "good risks" for a Brave New World regimen of medicants, electronic gadgets, and isolation chambers that would shift the locus and responsibility from the realm of corrections into that of the mental hospital. To the extent that there obtains very little support for maintenance of a category of "mental illness" called criminal sexual psychopathy created and maintained by serial acts of legislative group-think, the leadership of the mental health community might be on their side.

Surely, a decision to repeal the laws that legislatively prescribe treatment rather than punishment for sex offenders would win considerable political support from among the organized lobbies with which legislatures must contend; sex offenders have no such lobby, nor will many long argue that they deserve one. And that decision would come down smartly on the side of the "get tough, hang 'em high" posture that has won popular support in national elections.

To toss out the legislative intent to rehabilitate rather than punish would be to take a long step backwards across half a century. *But* (to return to the rumination for a last word), *in a curious way, repealing the laws that created the Twilight Zone in the first place might represent a more sensible (and perhaps even, if you'll pardon the term, "humane") decision than to continue to confine sex offenders segregated via unstable measures into an artificially distinct category as "treatable" rather than "punishable," especially when they are to be confined for treatment by methods that are so constrained as to be largely irrelevant to their rehabilitation.*

References

Abel, Gene, Donald J. Levis, & John Clancy. 1970. Aversion therapy applied to taped sequences of deviant behavior in exhibitionism and other sexual deviations. *Journal of Behaviour Therapy & Experimental Psychiatry*, 1, 59–66.

Abel, Gene, David H. Barlow, Edward B. Blanchard, & Donald Guild. 1977. The components of rapists' sexual arousal. *Archives of General Psychiatry*, 34, 895–903.

Albin, Rochelle S. 1977. Psychological studies of rape. *Signs*, 3, 423–435.

Alder, Christine. 1984. The convicted rapist: A sexual or a violent offender? *Criminal Justice & Behavior*, 11, 157–177.

Alexander, Cheryl S. 1980. The responsible victim: Nurses' perceptions of victims of rape. *Journal of Health & Social Behavior*, 21, 22–33.

American Psychiatric Association. 1952. *Diagnostic and Statistical Manual of Mental and Emotional Disorders*. Washington, DC: The Association.

American Psychiatric Association. 1974. *Clinical Aspects of the Violent Individual*. Washington, DC: The Association.

American Psychiatric Association. 1984. *Issues in Forensic Psychiatry*. Washington, DC: American Psychiatric Press.

American Psychiatric Association. 1987. *Diagnostic and Statistical Manual of Mental and Emotional Disorders, Third Edition, Revised*. Washington, DC: The Association.

American Psychological Association. 1978. Report of the task force on the role of psychology in the criminal justice system. *American Psychologist*, 33, 633–638.

Amick, Angelynne E., & Karen S. Calhoun. 1987. Resistance to sexual aggression: Personality, attitudinal, and situational factors. *Archives of Sexual Behavior*, 16, 153–164.

Amnesty International. 1987. *United States of America: The Death Penalty*. London: Amnesty International.

Anderson, Wayne P., Joseph T. Kunce, & Brice Rich. 1979. Sex offenders: Three personality types. *Journal of Clinical Psychology*, 35, 671–676.

Annis, Lawrence V. 1982. A residential treatment program for male sex offenders. *International Journal of Offender Therapy & Comparative Criminology*, 26, 223–234.

Annon, Jack S. 1988. Reliability and validity of penile plethysmography in rape and child molestation cases. *American Journal of Forensic Psychology*, 6, 11–26.

Appelbaum, Paul S. 1987. *Allen v. Illinois*: The Fifth Amendment and the sexually dangerous person. *Hospital & Community Psychiatry*, 38, 25–26.

Appelbaum, Paul S. 1988. The right to refuse treatment with antipsychotic medications: Retrospect and prospect. *American Journal of Psychiatry*, 145, 413–419.

Armentrout, James A., & Allen L. Hauer. 1978. MMPI's of rapists of adults, rapists of children, and non-rapist sex-offenders. *Journal of Clinical Psychology*, 34, 330–332.

Barker, E.T., & A.J. McLaughlin. 1977. Total encounter capsule. *Canadian Psychiatric Association Journal*, 22, 355–360.

Barlow, David H. 1973. Increasing heterosexual responsiveness in the treatment of sexual deviation: A review of the clinical and experimental evidence. *Behavior Therapy*, 4, 655–671.

Barlow, David H., Harold Leitenberg, & W. Stewart Agras. 1969. Experimental control of sexual deviation through manipulation of the noxious scene in covert sensitization. *Journal of Abnormal Psychology*, 74, 596–601.

Barnard, George W., Lynn Robbins, Gustave Newman, & Frank Carrera. 1984. A study of violence within a forensic treatment facility. *Bulletin of the American Academy of Psychiatry & the Law*, 12, 339–348.

Barnes, Gordon E., Neil M. Malamuth, & James V. Check. 1984. Psychoticism and sexual arousal to rape depictions. *Personality & Individual Differences*, 5, 273–279.

Barshis, Victoria G. 1983. The question of marital rape. *Women's Studies International Forum*, 6, 383–393.

Bauer, Herbert. 1983. Preparation of the sexually abused child for court testimony. *Bulletin of the American Academy of Psychiatry & the Law*, 11, 287–289.

Baum, Andrew, Robert J. Gatchel, & Marc A. Schaeffer. 1983. Emotional, behavioral, and physiological effects of chronic stress at Three Mile Island. *Journal of Consulting & Clinical Psychology*, 51, 565–572.

Baxter, David J., et al. 1984. Deviant sexual behavior: Differentiating sex offenders by criminal and personal history, psychometric measures, and sexual response. *Criminal Justice & Behavior*, 11, 477–501.

Baxter, D.J., H.E. Barbaree, & W.L. Marshall. 1986. Sexual responses to consenting and forced sex in a large sample of rapists and nonrapists. *Behaviour Research & Therapy*, 24, 513–520.

Beck, James C, Neal Borenstein, & Jennifer Dreyfus. 1986. The relationship between verdict, defendant characteristics, and type of crime in sex-related criminal cases. *Bulletin of the American Academy of Psychiatry & the Law*, 14, 141–146.

Becker, Judith V. 1984. Depressive symptoms associated with sexual assault. *Journal of Sex & Marital Therapy*, 10, 185–192.

Becker, Judith V., et al. 1982. The effects of sexual assault on rape and attempted rape victims. *Victimology*, 7, 106–113.

Becker, Judith V., & Linda J. Skinner. 1983. Assessment and treatment of rape-related sexual dysfunctions. *Clinical Psychologist*, 36, 102–105.

Becker, Judith V., Linda J. Skinner, Gene G. Abel, & Eileen G. Treacy. 1982. Incidence and types of sexual dysfunctions in rape and incest victims. *Journal of Sex & Marital Therapy*, 8, 65–74.

Becker, Judith V., Linda J. Skinner, Gene G. Abel, & Joan Cichon. 1984. Time limited therapy with sexually dysfunctional sexually assaulted women. *Journal of Social Work & Human Sexuality*, 3, 97–115.

Becker, Judith V., Meg S. Kaplan, Jerry Rathner Cunningham, & Richard Kavoussi. 1986. Characteristics of adolescent incest sexual perpetrators. *Journal of Family Violence*, 1, 85–97.

Beckham, Jean C, Lawrence V. Annis, & David L. Gustafson. 1989. Decision making and examiner bias in forensic expert recommendations for not guilty by reason of insanity. *Law & Human Behavior*, 13, 79–88.

Beech, H.R., Fraser Watts, & A. Desmond Poole. 1971. Classical conditioning of a sexual deviation. *Behavior Therapy*, 2, 400–402.

Beidelman, William. 1981. Group assertiveness training in correctional settings: A review and methodological critique. *Offender Rehabilitation*, 6, 69–87.

Beigel, Herbert. 1983. In defense of the insanity defense. *Hillside Journal of Clinical Psychiatry*, 5, 73–90.

Beit-Hallahmi, Benjamin. 1974. Treating the sex offender. *Crime & Delinquency*, 20, 33–37.

Belcastro, Philip A. 1982. A comparison of latent sexual behavior patterns between raped and never raped females. *Victimology*, 7, 224–230.

Bell, Carl C. 1986. Coma and the etiology of violence. *Journal of the National Medical Association*, 78, 1167–1176.

Berah, Ellen F., & Robert G. Myers. 1983. The offense records of a sample of convicted exhibitionists. *Bulletin of the American Academy of Psychiatry & the Law*, 11, 365–369.

Bergin, Allen E., & Michael J. Lambert. 1978. The evaluation of therapeutic outcomes. In Sol L. Garfield & Allen E. Bergin (eds.), *Handbook of Psychotherapy and Behavior Change*, 2d edition. New York: John Wiley. Pp. 437–490.

Bergner, Raymond M. 1987. Undoing degradation. *Psychotherapy*, 24, 25–30.

Berk, Richard A., Sarah F. Berk, & Phyllis J. Newton. 1984. Cops on call: Summoning the police to the scene of spousal violence. *Law & Society Review*, 18, 479–498.

Berliner, Lucy, & Doris Stevens. 1980. Advocating for sexually abused children in the criminal justice system. In Barbara M. Jones, Linda L. Jenstrom, & Kee MacFarlane (eds.), *Sexual Abuse of Children*. Washington, DC: National Center on Child Abuse & Neglect, U.S. Department of Health & Human Services. Pp. 47–50.

Berliner, Lucy, & Mary K. Barbieri. 1984. The testimony of the child victim in sexual assault. *Journal of Social Issues*, 40, 125–137.

Best, John B., & Herbert S. Demmin. 1982. Victim's provocativeness and victim's attractiveness as determinants of blame in rape. *Psychological Reports*, 51, 255–258.

Bicakova-Rocher, Alena, Michael H. Smolensky, Alain Reinberg, & Jean De Prins. 1985. Seasonal variations in socially and legally unacceptable sexual behavior. *Chronobiology International*, 2, 203–208.

Bidwell, Lee, & Priscilla White. 1986. The family context of marital rape. *Journal of Family Violence*, 1, 277–387.

Bienen, Leigh. 1983. Rape reform legislation in the United States: A look at some practical effects. *Victimology*, 8, 139–151.

Biggs, Faith H. 1987. Rape law in Massachusetts: Our Puritan forebearers and other cultural remnants. *New England Law Review*, 22, 89–130.

Blackburn, Ronald. 1975. Aggression and the EEG: A quantitative analysis. *Journal of Abnormal Psychology*, 84, 359–365.

Blackburn, Ronald. 1979. Cortical and autonomic arousal in primary and secondary psychopaths. *Psychophysiology*, 16, 143–150.

Bloom, Joseph D., John M. Bradford, & Lial Kofoed. 1988. An overview of psychiatric treatment approaches to three offender groups. *Hospital & Community Psychiatry*, 39, 151–158.

Boehnert, Caryl E. 1985. Psychological and demographic factors associated with individuals using the insanity defense. *Journal of Psychiatry & Law*, 13, 9–31.

Borgida, Eugene. 1981. Legal reform of rape laws. *Applied Social Psychology Annual*, 2, 211–241.

Borzecki, Mark, & J. Stephen Wormith. 1987. A survey of treatment programmes for sex offenders in North America. *Canadian Psychology*, 28, 30–44.

Boulton, Alan A., et al. 1983. Trace acid levels in the plasma and MAO activity in the platelets of violent offenders. *Psychiatry Research*, 8, 19–23.

Bowker, Lee H. 1983. Marital rape: A distinct syndrome? *Social Casework*, 64, 347–352.

Bradford, John M. 1983. The hormonal treatment of sexual offenders. *Bulletin of the American Academy of Psychiatry and the Law*, 11, 159–169.

Bradford, John M., & D. McLean. 1984. Sexual offenders, violence, and testosterone: A clinical study. *Canadian Journal of Psychiatry*, 29, 335–343.

Bradford, John M., & D. Bourget. 1987. Sexually aggressive men. *Psychiatric Journal of the University of Ottawa*, 12, 169–175.

Bradford, John M., & Anne Pawlak. 1987. Sadistic homosexual pedophilia: Treatment with cyproterone acetate. *Canadian Journal of Psychiatry*, 32, 22–30.

Bradmiller, Linda L., & William S. Walters. 1985. Seriousness of sexual assault charges: Influencing factors. *Criminal Justice & Behavior*, 12, 463–484.

Brant, R.S.T., & V.B. Tisza. 1977. The sexually misused child. *American Journal of Orthopsychiatry*, 47, 80–90.

Brecher, Edward M. 1978. *Treatment Programs for Sex Offenders*. Washington, DC: Law Enforcement Assistance Administration, U.S. Department of Justice.

Brett, Elizabeth A., Robert L. Spitzer, & Janet B.W. Williams. 1988. DSM-III-R criteria for posttraumatic stress disorder. *American Journal of Psychiatry*, 145, 1232–1236.

Briere, John, & Marsha Runtz. 1986. Suicidal thoughts and behaviours in former sexual abuse victims. *Canadian Journal of Behavioural Science*, 18, 413–423.

Briere, John, Neil Malamuth, & James V. Check. 1985. Sexuality and rape-supportive beliefs. *International Journal of Women's Studies*, 8, 398–403.

Brooks, Alexander D. 1986. The effect of law on the administration of antipsychotic medications. In Laurence Tancredi (ed.), *Ethical Issues in Epidemiologic Research*. New Brunswick: Rutgers University Press. Pp. 183–200.

Brunette, Stephen A., & Bruce Dennis Sales. 1980. The role of psychologists in state legislation governing sex offenders. *Professional Psychology*, 11, 194–201.

Bryant, Ernest T., Monte L. Scott, Christopher D. Tori, & Charles J. Golden. 1984. Neuropsychological deficits, learning disability, and violent behavior. *Journal of Consulting & Clinical Psychology*, 52, 323–324.

Bryer, Jeffrey B., Bernadette A. Nelson, Jean Baker Miller & Pamela A. Krol. 1987. Childhood sexual and physical abuse as factors in adult psychiatric illness. *American Journal of Psychiatry*, 144, 1426–1430.

Bulkley, Josephine. 1981. Other relevant child sexual abuse statutes: Domestic violence and sexual psychopath laws. In Josephine Bulkley (ed.), *Child Sexual Abuse and the Law*. Washington, DC: National Legal Resource Center for Child Advocacy and Protection, American Bar Association. Pp. 89–102.

Burgess, Ann Wolbert. 1983. Rape trauma syndrome. *Behavioral Sciences & the Law*, 1, 97–113.

Burgess, Ann Wolbert, & A. Nicholas Groth. 1980. Sexual victimization of children. In R. Volpe, M. Breton, & J. Mittion (eds.), *Maltreatment of the School-Aged Child*. Lexington, MA: D.C. Heath. Pp. 78–89.

Burgess, Ann Wolbert, Lynda Lytle Holmstrom, & Maureen P. McCausland. 1978. Divided loyalty in incest cases. In A.W. Burgess (ed.), *Sexual Assault of Children and Adolescents*. Lexington, MA: D.C. Heath. Pp. 115–126.

Burgess, Ann Wolbert, A. Nicholas Groth, & Maureen P. McCausland. 1981. Child sex initiation rings. *American Journal of Orthopsychiatry*, 51, 101–109.

Burgess, Ann Wolbert, Carol R. Hartman, & Arlene McCormack. 1987. Abused to abuser: Antecedents of socially deviant behaviors. *American Journal of Psychiatry*, 144, 1431–1436.

Burgess, Anthony. 1963. *A Clockwork Orange*. New York: Norton.

Bureau of the Census, U.S. Department of Commerce. 1989. *Statistical Abstract of the United States*. Washington, DC: U.S. Government Printing Office.

Burnett, Robbie C, Donald I. Templer, & Patrick C. Barker. 1985. Personality variables and circumstances of sexual assault predictive of a woman's resistance. *Archives of Sexual Behavior*, 14, 183–188.

Burt, Martha R. 1983. Justifying personal violence: A comparison of rapists and the general public. *Victimology*, 8, 131–150.

Bush, John M. 1983. Criminality and psychopathology: Treatment for the guilty. *Federal Probation*, 47, 44–49.

Calhoun, Karen S., Beverly M. Atkeson, & Patricia A. Resick. 1982. A longitudinal examination of fear reactions in victims of rape. *Journal of Counseling Psychology*, 29, 655–661.

Callahan, Edward J., & Harold Leitenberg. 1973. Aversion therapy for sexual deviation: Contingent shock and covert desensitization. *Journal of Abnormal Psychology*, 81, 60–73.

Caringella-MacDonald, Susan. 1985. Comparability in sexual and non-sexual assault case treatment: Did statute change meet the objective? *Crime & Delinquency*, 31, 206–222.

Caringella-MacDonald, Susan. 1988. Parallels and pitfalls: The aftermath of legal reform for sexual assault, marital rape, and domestic violence victims. *Journal of Interpersonal Violence*, 3, 174–189.

Carmen, Elaine H., Patricia P. Reiker, & Trudy Mills. 1984. Victims of violence and psychiatric illness. *American Journal of Psychiatry*, 141, 378–383.

Carson, David K., James R. Council, & Margaret A. Volk. 1988. Temperament, adjustment, and alcoholism in adult female incest victims. *Violence & Victims*, 3, 205–216.

Carson, David K., James R. Council, & Margaret A. Volk. 1989. Temperament as a predictor of psychological adjustment in female adult incest victims. *Journal of Clinical Psychology*, 45, 330–335.

Cavanaugh, James L., & Orest E. Wasyliw. 1985. Treating the not guilty by reason of insanity outpatient: A two-year study. *Bulletin of the American Academy of Psychiatry & the Law*, 13, 407–415.

Champion, Dean J. 1988. Child sexual abusers and sentencing severity. *Federal Probation*, 52, 53–57.

Chappell, Duncan. 1984. The impact of rape legislation reform: Some comparative trends. *International Journal of Women's Studies*, 7, 70–80.

Chiswick, Derek. 1987. Insanity in bar of trial in Scotland: A state hospital study. *British Journal of Psychiatry*, 132, 598–601.

Clarkin, John F., & Stephen W. Hurt. 1988. Psychological assessment: Tests and rating scales. In John A. Talbott, Robert E. Hales & Stuart C. Yudofsky (eds.), *The American Psychiatric Press Textbook of Psychiatry*. Washington, DC: American Psychiatric Press. Pp. 225–246.

Cluss, Patricia A., et al. 1983. The rape victim: Psychological correlates of participation in the legal process. *Criminal Justice & Behavior*, 10, 342–357.

Coates, Dan, & Tina Winston. 1983. Counteracting the deviance of depression: Peer support groups for victims. *Journal of Social Issues*, 39, 169–194.

Cocozza, J.J., & Henry J. Steadman. 1974. Some refinements in the measurement and prediction of dangerous behavior. *American Journal of Psychiatry*, 1974, 131, 1012–1014.

Cohen, Bruce M., Ferdinando Buonanno, Paul E. Keck, Seth P. Finkelstein, & Francine M. Benes. 1988. Comparison of MRI and CT scans in a group of psychiatric patients. *American Journal of Psychiatry*, 145, 1084–1088.

Cohen, Marcia I., Michael K. Spodak, Stuart B. Silver, & Katherine Williams. 1988. Predicting outcome of insanity acquittees released to the community. *Behavioral Sciences & the Law*, 6, 515–530.

Cohen, Murray L., Ralph Garofalo, Richard Boucher, & Theoharis Seghorn. 1977. The psychology of rapists. *Seminars in Psychiatry*, 3, 113–140.

Cohen, Theodore B., Eleanor Galenson, Kato van Leeuwen, & Brandt F. Steele. 1987. Sexual abuse in vulnerable and high risk children. *Child Abuse & Neglect*, 11, 461–474.

Colao, Flora, & Miriam Hunt. 1983. Therapists coping with sexual assault. *Women & Therapy*, 2, 205–214.

Comstock, George A. 1986. Sexual effects of movie and TV violence. *Medical Aspects of Human Sexuality*, 20, 96–101.

Conte, Jon R. 1985. Clinical dimensions of adult sexual abuse of children. *Behavioral Sciences & the Law*, 3, 341–354.

Coodley, Alfred. 1985. Psychodynamics of rapists. *American Journal of Forensic Psychiatry*, 6, 38–47.

Coons, Philip M. 1986. Child abuse and multiple personality disorder: Review of the literature and suggestions for treatment. *Child Abuse & Neglect*, 10, 455–472.

Coons, Philip M., & Victor Milstein. 1984. Rape and post-traumatic stress in multiple personality. *Psychological Reports*, 55, 839–845.

Coons, Philip M., & Victor Milstein. 1986. Psychosexual disturbances in multiple personality: Characteristics, etiology, and treatment. *Journal of Clinical Psychiatry*, 47, 106–110.

Cooper, Alan J. 1986. Progestogens in the treatment of male sex offenders: A review. *Canadian Journal of Psychiatry*, 31, 73–79.

Costell, Ronald M. 1980. The nature and treatment of male sex offenders. In Barbara M. Jones, Linda L. Jenstrom, & Kee MacFarlane (eds.), *Sexual Abuse of Children.* Washington, DC: National Center on Child Abuse & Neglect, U.S. Department of Health & Human Services. Pp. 29–30.

Covington, Stephanie S., & Janet Kohen. 1984. Women, alcohol, and sexuality. *Advances in Alcohol & Substance Abuse.* 4, 41–56.

Cowden, James. 1977. An evaluation of intensive group psychotherapy with male offenders in isolation units. *Corrective and Social Psychiatry*, 23, 69–72.

Crowe, Leif C., & William H. George. 1989. Alcohol and human sexuality: Review and integration. *Psychological Bulletin*, 105, 374–386.

Curran, William J. 1975. Confidentiality and the prediction of dangerousness in psychiatry. *New England Journal of Medicine*, 293, 285–286.

Curtis, John M. 1986. Factors in the sexual abuse of children. *Psychological Reports*, 58, 591–597.

Dabbs, James M., Robert L. Frady, Timothy S. Carr, & Norma F. Besch. 1987. Saliva testosterone and criminal violence in young adult prison inmates. *Psychosomatic Medicine*, 49, 174–182.

Damrosch, Shirley P. 1985. How perceived carelessness and time of attack affect nursing students' attributions about rape victims. *Psychological Reports*, 56, 531–536.

Danto, Bruce. 1985. *Identification and Control of Dangerous and Mentally Disordered Offenders*. Laguna Hills, CA: Eagle.

Davidson, Paul R., & P.B. Malcolm. 1985. The reliability of the rape index. *Behavioral Assessment*, 7, 283–292.

Davies, Allyson. 1979. Assessing outcomes of medical care: Some lessons for criminal offender rehabilitation. In Lee Sechrest, Susan O. White, & Elizabeth D. Brown, *The Rehabilitation of Criminal Offenders: Problems and Prospects*. Washington, DC: National Academy of Sciences. Pp. 151–162.

Davis, Bruce A., et al. 1983. Correlative relationships between biochemical activity and aggressive behavior. *Progress in Neuro-psychopharmacology & Biological Psychiatry*, 7, 529–535.

Davis, Glen E., & Harold Leitenberg. 1987. Adolescent sex offenders. *Psychological Bulletin*, 101, 417–427.

Deitz, Sheila R., Karen T. Blackwell, Paul C. Daley, & Brenda J. Bentley. 1982. Measurement of empathy toward rape victims and rapists. *Journal of Personality & Social Psychology*, 43, 372–384.

Deitz, Sheila R., Madeleine Littman, & Brenda J. Bentley. 1984. Attribution of responsibility for rape: The influence of observer empathy, victim resistance, and victim attractiveness. *Sex Roles*, 10, 261–280.

Dell, Susanne. 1983. The detention of diminished responsibility homicide offenders. *British Journal of Criminology*, 23, 50–60.

Dell, Susanne, & Alan Smith. 1983. Changes in the sentencing of diminished responsibility homicides. *British Journal of Psychiatry*, 142, 20–34.

Dembo, Richard, Max Dertke, Lawrence LaVoie, Scott Borders, et al. 1987. Physical abuse, sexual victimization, and illicit drug use: A structural analysis among high risk adolescents. *Journal of Adolescence*, 10, 13–34.

Denham, Priscilla L. 1982. Toward an understanding of child rape. *Journal of Pastoral Care*, 36, 235–245.

DeYoung, Mary. 1982. Innocent seducer and innocently seduced? The role of the child incest victim. *Journal of Child Clinical Psychology*, 11, 56–60.

DiMaria, Franco, & Santo DiNuovo. 1986. Judgments of aggression by Sicilian observers. *Journal of Social Psychology*, 126, 187–196.

DiVasto, Peter. 1985. Measuring the aftermath of rape. *Journal of Psychosocial Nursing & Mental Health Services*, 23, 33–35.

Dix, George E. 1976. Differential processing of abnormal sex offenders: Utilization of California's mentally disordered sex offender program. *Journal of Criminal Law & Criminology*, 67, 233–243.

Dix, George E. 1983. A legal perspective on dangerousness: Current status. *Psychiatric Annals*, 13, 243–256.

Donnerstein, Edward I., & Daniel G. Linz. 1986. Mass media, sexual violence, and male viewers: Current theory and research. *American Behavioral Scientist*, 29, 601–618.

Duffy, Clinton T., & Albert Hirshberg. 1965. *Sex and Crime*. Garden City: Doubleday.

Dutton, Wendy A., & Betty J. Newlon. 1988. Early recollections and sexual fantasies of adolescent sex offenders. *Individual Psychology*, 44, 85–94.

Dwyer, Margretta, & J. Ingrid Amberson. 1985. Sex offender treatment program: A follow-up study. *American Journal of Social Psychiatry*, 5, 56–60.

Earl, William L. 1985. Rape as a variable in marital therapy: Context and treatment. *Family Therapy*, 12, 259–272.

Earls, Christopher M., & Louis G. Castonguay. 1989. The evaluation of olfactory aversion for a bisexual pedophile with a single-case multiple baseline design. *Behavior Therapy*, 20, 137–146.

Earls, Christopher M., & Jean Proulx. 1986. The differentiation of Francophone rapists and non-rapists using penile circumferential measures. *Criminal Justice & Behavior*, 13, 419–429.

Eccles, A., W.L. Marshall, & H.E. Barbaree. 1988. The vulnerability of erectile measures to repeated assessments. *Behaviour Research & Therapy*, 26, 179–183.

Edwards, Susan. 1983. Sexuality, sexual offenses, and conceptions of victims in the criminal justice process. *Victimology*, 8, 113–130.

Einbender, Alison J., & William N. Friedrich. 1989. Psychological functioning and behavior of sexually abused girls. *Journal of Consulting & Clinical Psychology*, 57, 155–157.

Ellis, Elizabeth M. 1983. A review of empirical rape research: Victim reactions and response to treatment. *Clinical Psychology Review*, 3, 473–490.

Ellis, Elizabeth M., Beverly M. Atkeson, & Karen S. Calhoun. 1982. An examination of differences between multiple- and single-incident victims of sexual assault. *Journal of Abnormal Psychology*, 91, 221–224.

Elwell, Mary E., & Paul H. Ephross. 1987. Initial reactions of sexually abused children. *Social Casework*, 68, 109–116.

Erickson, William D., Michael G. Luxenberg, Nancy H. Walbek, & Richard K. Seely. 1987. Frequency of MMPI two point code types among sex offenders. *Journal of Consulting & Clinical Psychology*, 55, 566–570.

Esper, Jody. 1986. Reactions to violence: Normal adjustment is not psychopathology. *Issues in Radical Therapy*, 12, 25–27, 52–54.

Evans, D.R. 1968. Masturbatory fantasy and sexual deviation. *Behaviour Research & Therapy*, 6, 17–19.

Eysenck, H.J. 1964. *Crime and Personality*. London: Routledge & Kegan Paul.

Eysenck, H.J. 1966. *The Effects of Psychotherapy*. New York: International Science Press.

Eysenck, H.J. 1977. *Crime and Personality*, 2nd ed. London: Routledge & Kegan Paul.

Farkas, Gary M., & Raymond C. Rosen. 1976. Effects of alcohol on elicited male sexual response. *Journal of Studies on Alcohol*, 37, 265–272.

Farrall, William R. 1973. Selection and use of stimulus material for aversion therapy and desensitization. *Behavioral Engineering*, 1, 1–7.

Faulstich, Michael E. 1984. Effects of social perceptions of the insanity plea. *Psychological Reports*, 55, 183–187.

Faust, D., & J. Ziskin. 1988. The expert witness in psychology and psychiatry. *Science*, 241, 31–35.

Fehrenbach, Peter A., Wayne Smith, Caren Monastersky, & Robert Deisher. 1985. Adolescent sexual offenders: Offender and offense characteristics. *American Journal of Orthopsychiatry*, 56, 225–233.

Fein, Robert A. 1984. How the insanity acquittal retards treatment. *Law & Human Behavior*, 8, 283–292.

Feinstein, Anthony. 1989. Post-traumatic stress disorder: A descriptive study supporting *DSM-III-R* criteria. *American Journal of Psychiatry*, 146, 665–666.

Feldman, M.P., M.J. MacCulloch, & Mary L. MacCulloch. 1968. The aversion therapy treatment of a heterogeneous group of five cases of sexual deviation. *Acta Psychiatrica Scandinavica*, 44, 113–123.

Feldman, Robert S., & Linda F. Quenzer. 1984. *Fundamentals of Neuropsychopharmacology.* Sunderland, MA: Sinauer.

Feldman-Summers, Shirley, & Jeanette Norris. 1984. Differences between rape victims who report and those who do not report to a public agency. *Journal of Applied Social Psychology*, 14, 562–573.

Fersch, E.A. 1980. *Psychology and Psychiatry in Courts and Corrections: Controversy and Change.* New York: Wiley.

Fine, Michelle. 1983. Coping with rape: Critical perspectives on consciousness. *Imagination, Cognition & Personality*, 3, 249–267.

Finkel, Norman J., & Sharon F. Handel. 1989. How jurors construe "insanity." *Law & Human Behavior*, 13, 41–60.

Finkelhor, David. 1980. Sex among siblings: A survey on prevalence, variety, and effect. *Archives of Sexual Behavior*, 9, 171–194.

Finkelhor, David, & Kersti Yllo. 1982. Forced sex in marriage. *Crime & Delinquency*, 28, 459–478.

Finn, Jerry, & Julia Nile. 1984. A model for consolidating victim services. *Social Casework*, 65, 368–375.

Fiqia, Nasir A., Reuben A. Lang, Robert Plutchik, & Roger Holden. 1987. Personality differences between sex and violent offenders. *International Journal of Offender Therapy & Comparative Criminology*, 31, 211–216.

Fisher, Gary, & Lisla M. Howell. 1970. Psychological needs of homosexual pedophiliacs. *Diseases of the Nervous System*, 31, 623–625.

Flanagan, Timothy J., & Katherine M. Jamieson. 1988. *Sourcebook of Criminal Justice Statistics.* Washington, DC: Bureau of Justice Statistics, U.S. Department of Justice.

Flanagan, Timothy J., & Maureen McLeod. 1983. *Sourcebook of Criminal Justice Statistics.* Washington, DC: Bureau of Justice Statistics, U.S. Department of Justice.

Fookes, B.H. 1969. Some experiences in the use of aversion therapy in male homosexuality, exhibitionism, and fetishism-transvestism. *British Journal of Psychiatry*, 115, 339–341.

Forgac, Gregory E., & Edward J. Michaels, 1982. Personality characteristics of two types of male exhibitionists. *Journal of Abnormal Psychology*, 91, 287–293.

Forman, Bruce D., & J. Charles Wadsworth. 1985. Rape related services in Federally funded community mental health centers. *Journal of Community Psychology*, 13, 402–408.

Forrest, David V. 1987. Psychosocial treatment in neuropsychiatry. In Robert E. Hales & Stuart C. Yudofsky (eds.), *Textbook of Neuropsychiatry.* Washington, DC: American Psychiatric Press. Pp. 387–409.

Forst, M.L. 1978. *Civil Commitment and Social Control.* Lexington, MA: Heath.

Fowler, Raymond D. 1976. Sweeping reforms ordered in Alabama prisons. *American Psychological Association Monitor*, 7, 4, 1, 15.

Fowler, Raymond D. 1988. Assessment for decision in a correctional setting. In Donald R. Peterson & Daniel B. Fishman (eds.), *Assessment for Decision.* New Brunswick: Rutgers University Press. Pp. 214–239.

Frank, Ellen, & Barbara P. Anderson. 1987. Psychiatric disorders in rape victims: Past history and current symptomatology. *Comprehensive Psychiatry*, 28, 77–82.

Frank, Ellen, & Barbara D. Stewart. 1983. Treating depression in victims of rape. *Clinical Psychologist*, 36, 95–98.

Frank, Ellen, & Barbara D. Stewart. 1984. Depressive symptoms in rape victims: A revisit. *Journal of Affective Disorders*, 7, 77–85.

Frank, Julia B., Thomas R. Kosten, Earl L. Giller, Jr., & Elisheva Dan. 1988. A randomized clinical trial of phenelzine and impimpramine for posttraumatic stress disorder. *American Journal of Psychiatry*, 145, 1289–1291.

Frazier, Patricia, & Eugene Borgida. 1988. Juror common understanding and the admissibility of rape trauma syndrome evidence in court. *Law & Human Behavior*, 12, 101–122.

Fremouw, William J. 1976. A new right to treatment. In Stuart Golann & William J. Fremouw (eds.), *The Right to Treatment for Mental Patients.* New York: Irvington.

Freund, Kurt, & Ray Blanchard. 1986. The concept of courtship disorder. *Journal of Sex & Marital Therapy*, 12, 79–92.

Freund, Kurt, & Ray Blanchard. 1987. Feminine gender identity and physical aggressiveness in heterosexual and homosexual pedophiles. *Journal of Sex & Marital Therapy*, 13, 25–34.

Freund, Kurt, & Ray Blanchard. 1989. Phallometric diagnosis of pedophilia. *Journal of Consulting & Clinical Psychology*, 57, 100–105.

Freund, Kurt, Robin Watson, & Douglas Rienzo. 1988. Signs of feigning in the phallometric text. *Behaviour Research & Therapy*, 26, 105–112.

Friedman, Matthew J. 1988. Toward rational pharmacotherapy for posttraumatic stress disorder: An interim report. *American Journal of Psychiatry*, 145, 281–285.

Friedrich, William N., & William J. Luecke. 1988. Young school-age sexually aggressive children. *Professional Psychology*, 19, 155–164.

Frieze, Irene H. 1983. Investigating the causes and consequences of marital rape. *Signs*, 8, 532–553.

Furby, Lita, Mark R. Weinrott, & Lyn Blackshaw. 1989. Sex offender recidivism: A review. *Psychological Bulletin*, 105, 3–30.

Galliher, John F., & Cheryl Tyree. 1985. Edwin Sutherland's research on the origins of sexual psychopath laws: An early case of the medicalization of deviance. *Social Problems*, 33, 100–113.

Galski, Thomas, Kirtley E. Thornton, & David Shumsky. 1989. Brain damage in sex offenders. Unpublished. Kessler Institute for Rehabilitation Medicine, East Orange, NJ.

George, William H., Kurt H. Dermen, & Thomas H. Nochajski. 1989. Expectancy set, self-reported expectancies, and predispositional traits: Predicting interest in violence and erotica. *Journal of Studies on Alcohol*, 50, 541–551.

Giacopassi, David J., & Karen R. Wilkinson. 1985. Rape and the devalued victim. *Law & Human Behavior*, 9, 367–383.

Giannini, A. James, & Kay W. Fellows. 1986. Enhanced interpretation of nonverbal facial cues in male rapists. *Archives of Sexual Behavior*, 153–156.

Giarretto, Henry. 1980. Humanistic treatment of father-daughter incest. In Barbara M. Jones, Linda L. Jenstrom, & Kee MacFarlane (eds.), *Sexual Abuse of Children.* Washington, DC: National Center on Child Abuse & Neglect, U.S. Department of Health & Human Services. Pp. 39–46.

Gilmartin, Zena Pat. 1983. Attribution theory and rape victim responsibility. *Deviant Behavior*, 4, 357–374.

Girelli, Steven A., Patricia A. Resick, Susan Marhoefer-Dvorak, & Catherine K. Hutter. 1986. Subjective distress and violence during rape: Their effects on long-term fear. *Violence & Victims*, 1, 35–46.

Glaser, W.F. 1988. "Treatment" or "sentence" for child molestors: A comparison of Australian offenders with a general prison population. *International Journal of Law & Psychiatry*, 11, 145–156.

Glover, Benjamin. 1960. Control of the sex deviate. *Federal Probation*, 24, 38–45.

Golann, Stuart, & William J. Fremouw (eds.). 1976. *The Right to Treatment for Mental Patients*. New York: Irvington.

Goleman, Daniel. 1985. Violence against women in films. *Response to the Victimization of Women & Children*, 8, 21–22.

Gorenstein, Ethan E. 1982. Frontal lobe functions in psychopaths. *Journal of Abnormal Psychology*, 91, 368–379.

Gottfredson, Don M., & K.B. Ballard, Jr. 1966. Differences in parole decisions associated with decisionmakers. *Journal of Research in Crime & Delinquency*, 3, 112–118.

Gottfredson, Don M., Coleen A. Cosgrove, Leslie T. Wilkins, Judith Wallerstein, & Carol M. Rauh. 1978. *Classification for Parole Decision Policy*. Washington, DC: U.S. Government Printing Office.

Gottfredson, Don M., Leslie T. Wilkins, & Peter B. Hoffman. 1978. *Guidelines for Parole and Sentencing: A Policy Control Model*. Lexington, MA: Lexington Books.

Gottfredson, Michael R., & Don M. Gottfredson. 1980. *Decisionmaking in Criminal Justice: Toward the Rational Exercise of Discretion*. Cambridge, MA: Ballinger.

Grassian, Stuart, & Nancy Friedman. 1986. Effects of sensory deprivation in psychiatric seclusion and solitary confinement. *International Journal of Law & Psychiatry*, 8, 49–65.

Greendlinger, Virginia, & Donn Byrne. 1987. Coercive sexual fantasies of college men as predictors of self reported likelihood to rape and overt sexual aggression. *Journal of Sex Research*, 23, 1–11.

Greene, N.B. 1977. View of family pathology involving child molestation from a juvenile probation perspective. *Juvenile Justice*, 28, 29–34.

Greenland, Cyril. 1983. Sex law reform in international perspective: England and Wales and Canada. *Bulletin of the American Academy of Psychiatry & the Law*, 11, 309–330.

Greenland, Cyril. 1984. Dangerous sexual offender legislation in Canada, 1948–1977: An experiment that failed. *Canadian Journal of Criminology*, 26, 1–12.

Grier, Priscilla E. 1988. Cognitive problem-solving skills in antisocial rapists. *Criminal Justice & Behavior*, 15, 501–514.

Groff, Martin G. 1987. Characteristics of incest offenders' wives. *Journal of Sex Research*, 23, 91–96.

Groff, Martin G., & L.M. Hubble. 1984. A comparison of father-daughter and step-father-stepdaughter incest. *Criminal Justice & Behavior*, 11, 461–475.

Groth, A. Nicholas. 1978. Treatment of offenders. In *Research into Violent Behavior: Overview and Sexual Assaults*. Washington, DC: Committee on Science & Technology, U.S. House of Representatives.

Groth, A. Nicholas. 1979. *Men Who Rape: The Psychology of the Offender*. New York: Plenum.

Groth, A. Nicholas, & H. Jean Birnbaum. 1980. Adult sexual orientation and/attraction to underage persons. In Barbara M. Jones, Linda L. Jenstrom, & Kee MacFarlane (eds.), *Sexual Abuse of Children*. Washington, DC: National

Center on Child Abuse & Neglect, U.S. Department of Health & Human Services. Pp. 87–90.

Groth, A. Nicholas, & Ann W. Burgess. 1980. Male rape: Offenders and victims. *American Journal of Psychiatry*, 137, 806–810.

Groth, A. Nicholas, & William F. Hobson. 1983. The dynamics of sexual assault. In Louis B. Schlesinger & Eugene Revitch (eds.), *Sexual Dynamics of Anti-Social Behavior.* Springfield, IL: Thomas. Pp. 159–172.

Groth, A. Nicholas, Robert E. Longo, & J. Bradley McFadin. 1982. Undetected recidivism among rapists and child molesters. *Crime & Delinquency*, 28, 450–458.

Group for the Advancement of Psychiatry. 1950. *Psychiatrically Deviated Sex Offenders.* Topeka: The Group. Report No. 9.

Group for the Advancement of Psychiatry. 1954. *Criminal Responsibility and Psychiatric Expert Testimony.* Topeka: The Group, Report No. 26.

Group for the Advancement of Psychiatry. 1955. *Report on Homosexuality with Particular Emphasis on This Problem in Governmental Agencies.* Topeka: The Group, Report No. 30.

Group for the Advancement of Psychiatry. 1977, *Psychiatry and Sex Psychopath Legislation: The 30s to the 80s.* New York: Mental Health Materials, Publication No. 98.

Gruber, Kenneth J., Robert J. Jones, & Mary H. Freeman. 1982. Youth reactions to sexual assault. *Adolescence*, 17, 541–551.

Gundlach, R.H. 1977. Sexual molestation and rape reported by homosexual and heterosexual women. *Journal of Homosexuality*, 2, 367–384.

Gunn, John. 1976. Sexual offenders. *British Journal of Hospital Medicine*, 15, 57–58.

Gunn, John. 1982. An English psychiatrist looks at dangerousness. *Bulletin of the American Academy of Psychiatry and the Law*, 10, 143–153.

Hall, Eleanor R., Judith A. Howard, & Sherrie L. Boezio. 1986. Tolerance of rape: A sexist or antisocial attitude? *Psychology of Women Quarterly*, 10, 101–117.

Hall, Gordon C. 1988. Criminal behavior as a function of clinical and actuarial variables in a sexual offender population. *Journal of Consulting & Clinical Psychology*, 56, 773–775.

Hall, Gordon C. 1989-a. Self-reported hostility as a function of offense characteristics and response style in a sexual offender population. *Journal of Consulting & Clinical Psychology*, 57, 306–308.

Hall, Gordon C. 1989-b. Sexual arousal and arousability in a sexual offender population. *Journal of Abnormal Psychology*, 98, 145–149.

Hall, Gordon C., Roland D. Maiuro, Peter P. Vitaliano, & William C. Proctor. 1986. The utility of the MMPI with men who have sexually assaulted children. *Journal of Consulting & Clinical Psychology*, 54, 493–496.

Hall, Gordon C., & William C. Proctor. 1987. Criminological predictors of recidivism in a sexual offender population. *Journal of Consulting & Clinical Psychology*, 55, 111–112.

Hall, Gordon C., William C. Proctor, & George M. Nelson. 1988. Validity of physiological measures of pedophilic sexual arousal in a sexual offender population. *Journal of Consulting & Clinical Psychology*, 56, 118–122.

Hall, Harold V. 1982. Dangerousness predictions and the maligned forensic professional: Suggestions for detecting distortion of true basal violence. *Criminal Justice & Behavior*, 9, 3–12.

Hall, Harold V. 1984. Predicting dangerousness for the courts. *American Journal of Forensic Psychology*, 2, 5–25.

Hall, Harold V., & Frederick Lee Hall. 1987. Posttraumatic stress disorder as a legal defense in criminal trials. *American Journal of Forensic Psychology*, 5, 45–54.

Hall, Harold V., & Douglas McNinch. 1988. Linking crime-specific behavior to neuropsychological impairment. *International Journal of Clinical Neuropsychology*, 10, 113–122.

Hallam, R.S, & S. Rachman. 1972. Some effects of aversion therapy on patients with sexual disorders. *Behaviour Research & Therapy*, 10, 171–180.

Halleck, Seymour L. 1987. *The Mentally Disordered Offender.* Washington, DC: American Psychiatric Press.

Hanneke, Christine R., Nancy M. Shields, & George J. McCall. 1986. Assessing the prevalence of marital rape. *Journal of Interpersonal Violence*, 1, 350–362.

Hare, Robert D. 1985. Comparison of procedures for assessment of psychopathy. *Journal of Consulting & Clinical Psychology*, 53, 7–16.

Heath, Linda, Candace Kruttschnitt, & David Ward. 1986. Television and violent criminal behavior: Beyond the Bobo doll. *Violence and Victims*, 1, 177–190.

Heim, Nikolaus. 1981. Sexual behavior of castrated sex offenders. *Archives of Sexual Behavior*, 10, 11–19.

Heinrichs, Douglas W., & Robert W. Buchanan. 1988. Significance and meaning of neurological signs in schizophrenia. *American Journal of Psychiatry*, 145, 11–18.

Herman, Judith. 1983. Recognition and treatment of incestuous families. *International Journal of Family Therapy*, 5, 81–91.

Herman, Judith. 1986. Histories of violence in an outpatient population. *American Journal of Orthopsychiatry*, 56, 137–141.

Herman, Judith, & Emily Schatzow. 1984. Time-limited group therapy for women with a history of incest. *International Journal of Group Psychotherapy*, 34, 605–616.

Hobson, William F., Cheryl Boland, & Diane Jamieson. 1985. Dangerous sexual offenders. *Medical Aspects of Human Sexuality*, 19, 104–119.

Holland, T.R., G.E. Beckett, & N. Holt. 1982. Prediction of violent versus nonviolent recidivism from prior violent and nonviolent criminality. *Journal of Abnormal Psychology*, 91, 178–182.

Holland, T.R., G.E. Beckett, N. Holt, & M. Levi. 1983. Comparison and combination of clinical and statistical prediction of recidivism among adult offenders. *Journal of Applied Psychology*, 68, 203–211.

Holmes, Martha R., & Janet S. St. Lawrence. 1983. Treatment of rape-induced trauma: Proposed behavioral conceptualization and review of the literature. *Clinical Psychology Review*, 3, 417–433.

Holmstrom, Lynda Lytle, & Ann Wolbert Burgess. 1975. Rape: The victim and the criminal justice system. *International Journal of Criminology & Penology*, 3, 101–110.

Holmstrom, Lydna Lytle, & Ann Wolbert Burgess. 1983. *The Victim of Rape: Institutional Reactions.* New Brunswick: Transaction Books.

Howard, Richard C. 1984. The clinical EEG and personality in mentally abnormal offenders. *Psychological Medicine*, 14, 569–580.

Howard, R.C., & Charles R. Clark. 1985. When courts and experts disagree: Discordance between insanity recommendations and adjudications. *Law & Human Behavior*, 9, 385–396.

Howells, Kevin, & Eric Wright. 1978. The sexual attitudes of aggressive sexual offenders. *British Journal of Criminology*, 18, 170–174.

Howells, Kevin, et al. 1984. Perceptions of rape in a British sample: Effects of relationship, victim status, sex, and attitudes to women. *British Journal of Social Psychology*, 21, 35–40.

Hucker, S., R. Langevin, G. Wortzman, & J. Bain. 1986. Neuropsychological impairment in pedophiles. *Canadian Journal of Behavioural Science*, 18, 440–448.

Hunka, Carol D., Anita W. O'Toole, & Richard O'Toole. 1985. Self-help therapy in parents anonymous. *Journal of Psychosocial Nursing & Mental Health Services*, 23, 24–32.

Husain, Arshad, & James L. Chapel. 1983. History of incest in girls admitted to a psychiatric hospital. *American Journal of Psychiatry*, 140, 591–593.

Ingram, M. 1981. Participating victims: A study of sexual offenses with boys. In L.L. Constantine & F.M. Martinson (eds.), *Children and Sex: New Findings, New Perspectives.* Boston: Little, Brown. Pp. 177–187.

Jadhav, U.K. 1975. Laws on sex crimes. *Social Welfare*, 22, 26–28.

Jakimiec, J., F. Porporino, S. Addario, & C.D. Webster. 1986. Dangerous offenders in Canada, 1977–1985. *International Journal of Law & Psychiatry*, 9, 479–489.

James, David V. 1989. Child protection workers' role in erroneous allegations of child abuse. *American Journal of Psychiatry*, 146, 564.

Johnson, Shawn A., & Raymond E. Anderson. 1985. Development of scales to measure sexual aggressiveness. *International Journal of Offender Therapy & Comparative Criminology*, 29, 121–134.

Jortner, Sidney. 1985. To what degree was Freud wrong—and how much difference does it make? *Journal of Contemporary Psychotherapy*, 15, 114–122.

Juda, Daniel P. 1985. Psychoanalytically oriented crisis intervention and treatment of rape co-victims. *Dynamic Psychotherapy*, 3, 41–58.

Julian, Valerie, & Cynthia Mohr. 1979. Father/daughter incest: Profile of the offender. *Victimology*, 4, 348–360.

Kahn, Marvin W., & Lawrence Raifman. 1981. Hospitalization versus imprisonment and the insanity plea. *Criminal Justice & Behavior*, 8, 483–490.

Kalichman, Seth C, David Szymanowski, Geoffrey McKee, John Taylor, et al. 1989. Cluster analytically derived MMPI profile subgroups of incarcerated adult rapists. *Journal of Clinical Psychology*, 45, 149–155.

Kanekar, Suresh, & Laura Vaz. 1983. Determinants of perceived likelihood of rape and victim's fault. *Journal of Social Psychology*, 120, 147–148.

Kanekar, Suresh, Nirmala J. Pinto, & Deepa Mazumdar. 1985. Causal and moral responsibility of victims of rape and robbery. *Journal of Applied Social Psychology*, 15, 622–637.

Karasu, T. Byram, et al. 1989. *Treatments of Psychiatric Disorders: A Task Force Report of the American Psychiatric Association.* Washington, DC: American Psychiatric Press. Vols. I-IV.

Karuza, Jurgis, & Thomas O. Carey. 1984. Relative preference and adaptiveness of behavioral blame for observers of rape victims. *Journal of Personality*, 52, 249–260.

Kasper, C. James, Roger C. Baumann, & Jane Alford. 1984. Sexual abusers of children: The lonely kids. *Transactional Analysis Journal*, 14, 131–135.

Kavoussi, Richard J., Meg Kaplan, & Judith V. Becker. 1988. Psychiatric diagnoses in adolescent sex offenders. *Journal of the American Academy of Child & Adolescent Psychiatry*, 27, 241–243.

Kelley, Susan J. 1984. The use of art therapy with sexually abused children. *Journal of Psychosocial Nursing & Mental Health Services*, 22, 12–18.

Kelley, T.H., D.R. Cherek, & J.L. Steinberg. 1989. Concurrent reinforcement and alcohol: Interactive effects on human aggressive behavior. *Journal of Studies on Alcohol*, 50, 399–405.

Kilpatrick, Allie C. 1986. Some correlates of women's childhood sexual experiences: A retrospective study. *Journal of Sex Research*, 22, 221–242.

Kilpatrick, Dean G. 1983. Rape victims: Detection, assessment, and treatment. *Clinical Psychologist*, 36, 92–95.

Kilpatrick, Dean G., Connie L. Best, Lois J. Veronen, Angelynne E. Amick, Lorenz A. Villeponteaux, & Gary A. Ruff. 1985. Mental health correlates of criminal victimization: A random community survey. *Journal of Consulting & Clinical Psychology*, 53, 866–873.

Kirkland, Karen D., & Chris A. Bauer. 1982. MMPI traits of incestuous fathers. *Journal of Clinical Psychology*, 38, 645–649.

Knight, Raymond A., & Robert A. Prentky. 1987. The developmental antecedents and adult adaptations of rapist subtypes. *Criminal Justice & Behavior*, 14, 403–426.

Koss, Mary P., & Cheryl J. Oros. 1982. Sexual experiences survey: A research instrument investigating sexual aggression and victimization. *Journal of Consulting & Clinical Psychology*, 50, 455–457.

Koss, Mary P., Kenneth E. Leonard, Dana A. Beezley, & Cheryl J. Oros. 1985. Nonstranger sexual aggression: A discriminant analysis of the psychological characteristics of undetected offenders. *Sex Roles*, 12, 981–992.

Kozma, Carolyn, & Marvin Zuckerman. 1983. An investigation of some hypotheses concerning rape and murder. *Personality & Individual Differences*, 4, 23–29.

Kozol, H., R. Boucher, & R. Garofalo. 1972. The diagnosis and treatment of dangerousness. *Crime and Delinquency*, 18, 371–392.

Kraulewitz., Judith E. 1982. Reactions to rape victims: Effects of rape circumstances, victim's emotional response, and sex of helper. *Journal of Counseling Psychology*, 29, 645–654.

Kutash, Irwin L. 1984. Aggression victimology: Treatment of the victim. *Current Issues in Psychoanalytic Practice*, 1, 47–64.

LaFree, Gary D., Barbara F. Reskin, & Christy A. Visher. 1985. Jurors' responses to victims' behavior and legal issues in sexual assault trials. *Social Problems*, 32, 389–407.

LaGuardia, Robert L., Glenn Smith, Robert Francois, and Lea Bachman. 1983. Incidence of delayed stress disorder among Vietnam era veterans: The effect of priming on response set. *American Journal of Orthopsychiatry*, 53, 18–27.

Lamb, H. Richard, Linda E. Weinberger, & Bruce H. Gross. 1988. Court-mandated community outpatient treatment for persons found not guilty by reason of insanity: A five-year follow-up. *American Journal of Psychiatry*, 145, 450–456.

Lang, Reuben A., Chris A. Lloyd, & Nasir A. Fiqia. 1985. Goal attainment scaling with hospitalized sexual offenders. *Journal of Nervous & Mental Disease*, 173, 527–537.

Langenluddeke, Adolf. 1965. Die behandlung von sittlichkeitsverbrechern. *Soziale Arbeit*, 14,101–110.

Langevin, Ron, Mark Ben-Aron, George Wortzman, & Robert Dickey. 1987. Brain damage, diagnosis, and substance abuse among violent offenders. *Behavioral Sciences & the Law*, 5, 77–94.

Lanyon, Richard, & Robert W. Lutz. 1984. MMPI discrimination of defensive and non-defensive felony sex offenders. *Journal of Consulting & Clinical Psychology*, 52, 841–843.

Larmand, K., & Albert Pepitone. 1982. Judgments of rape: A study of victimrapist relationship and victim sexual history. *Personality & Social Psychology Bulletin*, 8, 134–139.

Laws, D.R. 1980. Treatment of bisexual pedophilia by a biofeedback-assisted self-control procedure. *Behaviour Research & Therapy*, 18, 207–211.

LeBeau, James L. 1984. Rape and racial patterns. *Journal of Offender Counseling, Services & Rehabilitation*, 9, 125–148.

LeBeau, James L. 1988. Statute revision and the reporting of rape. *Sociology & Social Research*, 72, 201–207.

Lemmon, Kenneth W. 1984. Hypnoanalytic art therapy with victims of rape and incest. *Medical Hypnoanalysis*, 6, 104–108.

Lenox, Michelle C., & Linda R. Gannon. 1983. Psychological consequences of rape and variables influencing recovery: A review. *Women & Therapy*, 1, 37–49.

Levin, Saul M., & Lawrence Stava. 1987. Personality characteristics of sex offenders: A review. *Archives of Sexual Behavior*, 16, 57–79.

Levine-MacCombie, Joyce, & Mary P. Koss. 1986. Acquaintance rape: Effective avoidance strategies. *Psychology of Women Quarterly*, 10, 311–319.

Lidberg, Lars. 1985. Platelet monoamine oxidase activity and psychopathy. *Psychiatry Research*, 16, 339–343.

Linz, Daniel G., Edward Donnerstein, & Steven Penrod. 1984. The effects of multiple exposures to filmed violence against women. *Journal of Communication*, 34, 130–147.

Lipton, Ronald M., Elizabeth C. McDonnell, & Richard M. McFall. 1987. Heterosocial perception in rapists. *Journal of Consulting & Clinical Psychology*, 55, 17–21.

Litwack, Thomas R., & Louis B. Schlesinger. 1987. Assessing and predicting violence: Research, law, and applications. In Irving B. Weiner & Allen K. Hess (eds.), *Handbook of Forensic Psychology*. New York: Wiley. Pp. 205–257.

Loh, Wallace D. 1981. Q: What has reform of rape legislation wrought? A: Truth in criminal labelling. *Journal of Social Issues*, 37, 28–52.

Longo, Robert E. 1982. Sexual learning and experiences among adolescent sexual offenders. *International Journal of Offender Therapy & Comparative Criminology*, 26, 235–241.

Lowrie, Mattie. 1987. Adult survivors of childhood incest. *Journal of Psychosocial Nursing & Mental Health Services*, 25, 27–31.

Luckey, James W., & John J. Berman. 1981. Effects of new commitment laws on the mental health system. *American Journal of Orthopsychiatry*, 51, 479–483.

Lutz, Susan E., & Joan P. Medway. 1984. Contextual family therapy for the victims of incest. *Journal of Adolescence*, 7, 319–337.

Luxenberg, Jay S., Susan E. Swedo, Martine F. Flament, Robert P. Friedland, Judith Rapoport, & Stanley L. Rapoport. 1988. Neuroanatomical abnormalities in obsessive compulsive disorder detected with quantitative X-ray computed tomography. *American Journal of Psychiatry*, 145, 1089–1093.

Lystad, Mary H. 1982. Sexual abuse in the home: A review of the literature. *International Journal of Family Psychiatry*, 3, 3–31.

MacCulloch, M.J., C. Williams, & C.J. Birtles. 1971. The successful application of aversion therapy to an adolescent exhibitionist. *Journal of Behaviour Therapy & Experimental Psychiatry*, 2, 61–66.

MacDonald, George J. 1971. *Community Adjustment of Treated Sexual Offenders*. Fort Steilacoom: Western State Hospital, State of Washington.

Madlafousek, J., A. Kolarovsky, & J. Zverina. 1985. Penile volume response to female emotional behavior in men committing forcible sexual acts. *Activitas Nervosa Superior*, 27, 151–152.

Malamuth, Neil M. 1986. Predictors of naturalistic sexual aggression. *Journal of Personality & Social Psychology*, 50, 953–962.

Malamuth, Neil M. 1988. Predicting laboratory aggression against female and male targets: Implications for sexual aggression. *Journal of Research in Personality*, 22, 474–495.

Malamuth, Neil M., & John Briere. 1986. Sexual violence in the media: Indirect effects on aggression against women. *Journal of Social Issues*, 42, 75–92.

Malamuth, Neil M., & Joseph Centi. 1986. Repeated exposure to violent and non-violent pornography: Likelihood of raping ratings and laboratory aggression against women. *Aggressive Behavior*, 12, 129–137.

Malamuth, Neil M., & James V. Check. 1985. The effects of aggressive pornography on beliefs in rape myths: Individual differences. *Journal of Research in Personality*, 19, 299–320.

Malamuth, Neil M., Maggie Heim, & Seymour Feshbach. 1980. Sexual responsiveness of college students to rape depictions. *Journal of Personality & Social Psychology*, 38, 399–408.

Malcolm, P.B., P.R. Davidson, & W.L. Marshall. 1985. Control of penile tumescence: The effects of arousal level and stimulus content. *Behaviour Research & Therapy*, 23, 273–280.

Malloy, Paul F., John A. Fairbank, & Terence M. Keane. 1983. Validation of a multimethod assessment of posttraumatic stress disorders in Vietnam veterans. *Journal of Consulting & Clinical Psychology*, 51, 488–494.

Malmquist, Carl P. 1985. Sexual offenses among adolescents. *Medical Aspects of Human Sexuality*, 19, 134–139.

Marks, Isaac, Michel Gelder, & John Bancroft. 1970. Sexual deviants two years after electric aversion. *British Journal of Psychiatry*, 117, 173–185.

Marolla, Joseph A., & Diana Scully. 1986. Attitudes toward women, violence, and rape: A comparison of convicted rapists and other felons. *Deviant Behavior*, 7, 337–355.

Marshall, Peter G., Alfred A. Keltner, & William L. Marshall. 1981. Anxiety reduction, assertiveness training, and enactment of consequences: A comparative treatment study in the modification of non-assertion and social fear. *Behavior Modification*, 5, 85–102.

Marshall, W.L. 1973. The modification of sexual fantasies: A combined treatment approach to the reduction of deviant sexual behavior. *Behavior Research & Therapy*, 11, 557–564.

Marshall, W.L., & R.D. McKnight. 1975. An integrated treatment program for sexual offenders. *Canadian Psychiatric Association Journal*, 20, 133–138.

Marshall, W.L., H.E. Barbaree, & Jennifer Burt. 1988. Sexual offenders against male children. *Behavior Research & Therapy*, 26, 383–391.

Marshall, W.L., H.E. Barbaree, & D. Christophe. 1986. Sexual offenders against female children: Sexual preferences for age of victims and type of behavior. *Canadian Journal of Behavioural Science*, 18, 424–439.

Marvasti, Jamshid. 1985. Fathers who commit incest: Jail or treatment? Need for a "victim-oriented law." *American Journal of Forensic Psychiatry*, 6, 8–13.

Matek, Ord. 1985. The use of fantasy training as a therapeutic process in working with sexual offenders. *Journal of Social Work & Human Sexuality*, 4, 109–123.

McDonald, Angus, & Daniel Paitich. 1981. A study of homicide: The validity of predictive test factors. *Canadian Journal of Psychiatry*, 1981, 26, 549–554.

McDonald, Angus, & Daniel Paitich. 1982–83. Psychological profile of the rapist. *American Journal of Forensic Psychiatry*, 3, 159–172.

McGarrell, Edmund F., & Timothy J. Flanagan. 1985. *Sourcebook of Criminal Justice Statistics.* Washington, DC: Bureau of Justice Statistics, U.S. Department of Justice.

McGaughey, Karen J., & William B. Stiles. 1983. Courtroom interrogation of rape victims: Verbal response mode use by attorneys and witnesses during direct examination vs. cross-examination. *Journal of Applied Social Psychology*, 13, 78–87.

Medlicott, R.W. 1976. Psychiatric aspects of murder and attempted murder. *New Zealand Medical Journal*, 83, 5–9.

Megargee, Edwin 1.1970. The prediction of violence with psychological tests. In Charles S. Spielberger (ed.), *Current Topics in Clinical and Community Psychiatry.* New York: Academic Press.

Melton, Gary B. 1984. Child witnesses and the First Amendment: A psycholegal dilemma. *Journal of Social Issues*, 40, 109–123.

Menzies, Robert J., Christopher D. Webster, & Diana S. Sepejak. 1985. The dimensions of dangerousness: Evaluating the accuracy of psychometric predictions of violence among forensic patients. *Law & Human Behavior*, 9, 49–70.

Michael, Richard P., & Doris Zumpe. 1983-a. Annual rhythms in human violence and sexual aggression in the United States and the role of temperature. *Social Biology*, 30, 263–278.

Michael, Richard P., & Doris Zumpe. 1983-b. Sexual violence in the United States and the role of season. *American Journal of Psychiatry*, 140, 883–886.

Miller, Robert D., Gary J. Maier, Frederick W. Blancke, & Dennis Doren. 1986. Litigiousness as a resistance to therapy. *Journal of Psychiatry & Law*, 14, 109–123.

Miller, Robert D., Lawrence J. Stava, & Rodney K. Miller. 1988. The insanity defense for sex offenders: Jury decisions after repeal of Wisconsin's sex crimes law. *Hospital & Community Psychiatry*, 39, 186–189.

Mitchell, Chester N. 1986. Culpable mental disorder and criminal liability. *International Journal of Law & Psychiatry*, 8, 273–299.

Mitra, Charlotte L. 1987. Judicial discourse in father-daughter incest appeal cases. *International Journal of the Sociology of the Law*, 15, 121–148.

Monahan, John. 1976. The prediction of violence. In John Monahan (ed.), *Community Mental Health and the Criminal Justice System.* New York: Pergamon. Pp. 13–34.

Monahan, John. 1981-a. *The Clinical Prediction of Violent Behavior.* Washington, DC: U.S. Department of Health & Human Services.

Monahan, John. 1981-b. *Predicting Violent Behavior: An Assessment of Clinical Techniques.* Beverly Hills: Sage.

Monahan, John. 1983. The prediction of violent behavior: Developments in psychology and law. In C. James Scheirer & Barbara L. Hammonds (eds.), *Psychology and the Law.* Washington, DC: American Psychological Association. Pp. 147–176.

Money, John, & June Werlwas. 1982. Paraphilic sexuality and child abuse: The parents. *Journal of Sex & Marital Therapy*, 8, 57–64.

Morrison, James C. 1989. Childhood sexual histories of women with somatization disorder. *American Journal of Psychiatry*, 146, 239–241.

Mosher, Donald L., & Ronald D. Anderson. 1986. Macho personality, sexual aggression, and reactions to guided imagery of realistic rape. *Journal of Research in Personality*, 20, 77–94.

Moss, Gene R., Richard T. Rada, & James B. Appel. 1970. Positive control as an alternative to aversion therapy. *Journal of Behavior Therapy & Experimental Psychiatry*, 1, 291–294.

Mueller, Gerhard O.W. 1961. The public law of wrongs—Its concepts in the world of reality. *Journal of Public Law*, 10, 203–244.

Mullen, P.E. 1984. Mental disorder and dangerousness. *Australian and New Zealand Journal of Psychiatry*, 18, 8–17.

Murphy, William D., Emily M. Coleman, & Mary R. Haynes. 1986. Factors related to coercive sexual behavior in a non-clinical sample of males. *Violence & Victims*, 1, 255–278.

Murphy, William D., Joseph Krisak, Susan Stalgaitis, & Karen Anderson. 1984. The use of penile tumescence measures with incarcerated rapists: Further validity issues. *Archives of Sexual Behavior*, 13, 545–554.

Myers, Martha A., & Gary D. LaFree. 1982. Sexual assault and its prosecution: A comparison with other crimes. *Journal of Criminal Law & Criminology*, 73, 1282–1305.

Myers, Mary B., Donald I. Templer, & Ric Brown. 1984. Coping ability in women who become victims of rape. *Journal of Consulting & Clinical Psychology*, 52, 73–78.

Myers, Thomas J. 1965. Psychiatric examination of the sexual psychopath. *Journal of Criminal Law, Criminology & Police Science*, 56, 27–31.

Nacci, Peter L., & Thomas R. Kane. 1984. Inmate sexual aggression: Some evolving propositions, empirical findings, and mitigating counter-forces. *Journal of Offender Counseling, Services & Rehabilitation*, 9, 1–20.

National Center for State Courts, U.S. Department of Justice. 1979. *State Court Caseload Statistics.* Washington, DC: National Criminal Justice Statistics and Information Service.

Nezu, Arthur M., & George F. Roman. 1985. Life stress, current problems, problem solving, and depressive symptoms: An integrative model. *Journal of Consulting & Clinical Psychology*, 1985, 693–697.

Nicholson, Robert A. 1988. Validation of a brief form of the Competency Screening Test. *Journal of Clinical Psychology*, 44, 87–90.

O'Brien, Robert M. 1987. The interracial nature of violent crimes: A re-examination. *American Journal of Sociology*, 92, 817–835.

O'Hare, Janet, & Katy Taylor. 1983. The reality of incest. *Women & Therapy*, 2, 215–229.

Oliver, Anthony D. 1982. The sex offender: Lessons from the California experience. *International Journal of Law & Psychiatry*, 5, 403–411.

Oliver, Anthony D. 1982–83. The mentally disordered sex offender: Facts and fictions. *American Journal of Forensic Psychiatry*, 3, 87–99.

Orlando, James A., & Mary P. Koss. 1983. The effects of sexual victimization on sexual satisfaction: A study of the negative-association hypothesis. *Journal of Abnormal Psychology*, 92, 104–106.

Overholser, James C, & Steven Beck. 1986. Multimethod assessment of rapists, child molesters, and three control groups on behavioral and psychological measures. *Journal of Consulting & Clinical Psychology*, 54, 682–687.

Owens, Travis H. 1984. Personality traits of female psychotherapy patients with a history of incest. *Journal of Personality Assessment*, 48, 606–608.

Pacht, Asher R., & James E. Cowden. 1974. An exploratory study of five hundred sex offenders. *Criminal Justice & Behavior*, 1, 13–20.

Pacifico, J. Franklin, & Stuart Brown. 1988. Polygraph and plethysmograph: Improvements in "state of the art" technology in the clinical assessment and treatment of the sexual offender. Fourth Annual Symposium, American College of Forensic Psychology, Palm Springs.

Pallak, Suzanne R., & Jacqueline M. Davies. 1982. Finding fault versus attributing responsibility: Using facts differently. *Personality & Social Psychology Bulletin*, 8, 454–459.

Pallone, Nathaniel J. 1986. *On the Social Utility of Psychopathology: A Deviant Majority and Its Keepers?* New Brunswick: Transaction Books.

Pandina, Robert J. 1989. Preliminary notes for a paradigm linking alcohol, sex, and aggression. Unpublished. Center for Alcohol Studies, Rutgers University.

Pankratz, Loren D. 1984. Murder and insanity: 19th century perspectives from the "American Journal of Insanity." *International Journal of Offender Therapy & Comparative Criminology*, 28, 37–43.

Panton, J.H. 1978. Personality differences between rapists of adults, rapists of children, and non-violent sexual molesters of female children. *Research Communications in Psychology, Psychiatry & Behavior*, 3, 385–393.

Panton, J.H. 1979. MMPI profile configurations associated with incestuous and non-incestuous child molesting. *Psychological Reports*, 45, 335–338.

Papen, James H. 1988. Forensic psychological evaluation and report: Child sexual molestation: Assessment for dangerousness potential. *American Journal of Forensic Psychology*, 6, 23–41.

Pardeck, John T., & Wesley L. Nolden. 1985. An evaluation of a crisis intervention center for parents at risk. *Family Therapy*, 12, 25–33.

Parisi, Nicolette, Michael R. Gottfredson, Michael J. Hindelang, & Timothy J. Flanagan. 1979. *Sourcebook of Criminal Justice Statistics.* Washington, DC: Bureau of Justice Statistics, U.S. Department of Justice.

Parker, Hilda, & Seymour Parker. 1986. Father/daughter sexual abuse: An emerging perspective. *American Journal of Orthopsychiatry*, 56, 531–549.

Pasewark, R.A., M.L. Pantile, & Henry J. Steadman. 1979. Characteristics and disposition of persons found not guilty by reason of insanity in New York state, 1971–76. *American Journal of Psychiatry*, 136, 655–660.

Peretti, Peter O., & Nancy Cozzens. 1983. Characteristics of female rapees not reporting and reporting the first incidence of rape. *Corrective & Social Psychiatry & Journal of Behavior Technology, Methods & Therapy*, 29, 82–87.

Perry, Josephus D., & Miles E. Simpson. 1987. Violent crimes in a city: Environmental determinants. *Environment & Behavior*, 19, 77–90.

Petrovich, Michael, & Donald I. Templer. 1984. Heterosexual molestation of children who later become rapists. *Psychological Reports*, 54, 810.

Phillips, Michael R., Aron S. Wolf, & David J. Coons. 1988. Psychiatry and the criminal justice system: Testing the myths. *American Journal of Psychiatry*, 145, 605–610.

Pierce, Lois H., & Robert L. Pierce. 1984. Race as a factor in the sexual abuse of children. *Social Work Research*, 20, 9–14.

Pierce, Lois H., & Robert L. Pierce. 1987. Incestuous victimization by juvenile sex offenders. *Journal of Family Violence*, 2, 351–354.

Pierce, Robert L., & Lois H. Pierce. 1985. The sexually abused child: A comparison of male and female victims. *Child Abuse & Neglect*, 9, 191–199.

Ploughman, Penelope, & John Stensrud. 1986. The ecology of rape victimization: A case study of Buffalo, New York. *Genetic, Social & General Psychology Monographs*, 112, 303–324.

Plummer, Diane L., Jack O. Jenkins, & Leonard Hampton. 1984. Rape and intervention strategies. *Crisis Intervention*, 13, 104–113.

Poitrast, F.G. 1976. The judicial dilemma in child abuse cases. *Psychiatric Opinion*, 13, 23–28.

Prentky, Robert A., & Daniel L. Carter. 1984. The predictive value of the triad for sex offenders. *Behavioral Sciences & the Law*, 2, 341–354.

Prentky, Robert A., & Raymond A. Knight. 1986. Impulsivity in the lifestyle and criminal behavior of sexual offenders. *Criminal Justice & Behavior*, 13, 141–164.

Prentky, Robert A., Murray Cohen, & Theoharis Seghorn. 1985. Development of a rational taxonomy for the classification of rapists: The Massachusetts Treatment Center system. *Bulletin of the American Academy of Psychiatry & the Law*, 13, 39–70.

Price, Gail M. 1985. Fathers, provoke not your children: A study of rage in a sexually abused girl. *Journal of Psychology & Christianity*, 4, 71–75.

Pugh, M.D. 1983. Contributory fault and rape convictions: Loglinear models for blaming the victim. *Social Psychology Quarterly*, 46, 233–242.

Quinsey, Vernon L. 1973. Methodological issues in evaluating the effectiveness of aversion therapies for institutionalized child molesters. *Canadian Psychologist*, 14, 350–361.

Quinsey, Vernon L. 1983. Prediction of recidivism and the evaluation of treatment programs for sex offenders. In Simon N. Verdun-Jones & Alfred A. Keltner (eds.), *Sexual Aggression and the Law*. Burnaby, BC: Criminologic Research Centre, Simon Fraser University. Pp. 27–40.

Quinsey, Vernon L., & Terry C. Chaplin. 1982. Penile responses to nonsexual violence among rapists. *Criminal Justice & Behavior*, 9, 372–381.

Quinsey, Vernon L., & Terry C. Chaplin. 1984. Stimulus control of rapists' and non-sex offenders' sexual arousal. *Behavioral Assessment*, 6, 169–176.

Quinsey, Vernon L., & Anne Maguire. 1986. Maximum security psychiatric patients: Actuarial and clinical predictions of dangerousness. *Journal of Interpersonal Violence*, 1, 143–171.

Quinsey, Vernon L., & Douglas Upfold. 1985. Rape completion and victim injury as a function of female resistance strategy. *Canadian Journal of Behavioural Science*, 17, 40–50.

Quinsey, Vernon L., Terry C. Chaplin, & Douglas Upfold. 1984. Sexual arousal to non-sexual violence and sadomasochistic themes among rapists and non-sex offenders. *Journal of Consulting & Clinical Psychology*, 52, 651–657.

Rachlin, Stephen, Abraham L. Halpern, & Stanley L. Portnow. 1984. The volitional rule, personality disorders, and the insanity defense. *Psychiatric Annals*, 14, 139–141, 145–147.

Rachman, Stanley, & John Teasdale. 1969. *Aversion Therapy and Behaviour Disorders: An Analysis.* Coral Gables, FL: University of Miami Press.

Rachman, S.J., & G.T. Wilson. 1980. *The Effects of Psychological Therapy*, 2nd edition. Oxford: Pergamon.

Rada, Richard, & Robert Kellner. 1976. Plasma testosterone levels in the rapist. *Psychosomatic Medicine*, 38, 257–268.

Rada, Richard, D.R. Laws, Robert Kellner, Laxmi Stivasta, & Glenn Peake. 1983. Plasma androgens in violent and non-violent sex offenders. *Bulletin of the American Academy of Psychiatry & the Law*, 11, 149–158.

Rader, Charles M. 1977. MMPI profile types of exposers, rapists, and assaulters in a court services population. *Journal of Consulting & Clinical Psychology*, 45, 61–69.

Raiha, Nancy K. 1983. Comprehensive care for the victim of sexual assault. *Military Medicine*, 148, 796–799.

Randolph, M. Kay, & Gilbert R. Gredler. 1985. Prevention of child sexual assault. *Casework Techniques*, 1, 399–402.

Raymond, Michael J. 1967. Treatment by revulsion. *Mental Health*, 26, 24–25.

Reinehr, Robert C., Harold K. Dudley, & John V. White. 1985. Dangerousness review boards: Their composition and their functions. *Journal of Psychiatry & Law*, 13, 449–456.

Reitz, Willard E., & William E. Keil. 1971. Behavioral treatment of an exhibitionist. *Journal of Behavior Therapy & Experimental Psychiatry*, 2, 67–69.

Renner, K. Edward, & Suresh Sahjpaul. 1986. The new sexual assault law: What has been its effect? *Canadian Journal of Criminology*, 28, 407–413.

Reppucci, N. Dickon, & Jeffrey J. Haugaard. 1989. Prevention of child sexual abuse: Myth or reality? *American Psychologist*, 44, 1266–1275.

Resick, Patricia A. 1983. The rape reaction: Research findings and implications for intervention. *Behavior Therapist*, 6, 129–132.

Resick, Patricia A., Karen S. Calhoun, Beverly M. Atkeson, & Elizabeth M. Ellis. 1981. Social adjustment in victims of sexual assault. *Journal of Consulting & Clinical Psychology*, 49, 705–712.

Ressler, Robert K., Ann W. Burgess, & John E. Douglas. 1983. Rape and rape-murder: One offender and twelve victims. *American Journal of Psychiatry*, 140, 36–40.

Revitch, Eugene. 1983. Burglaries with sexual dynamics. In Louis B. Schlesinger & Eugene Revitch (eds.), *Sexual Dynamics of Anti-Social Behavior*. Springfield, IL: Thomas. Pp. 173–191.

Revitch, Eugene, & Louis B. Schlesinger. 1989. *Sex Murder and Sex Aggression: Phenomenology, Psychopathology, Psychodynamics, and Prognosis.* Springfield, IL: Thomas.

Reynolds, Lynn. 1984. Rape: A social perspective. *Journal of Offender Counseling, Services & Rehabilitation*, 1984, 149–160.

Rezmovic, Eva. 1979. Methodological considerations in evaluating correctional effectiveness: Issues and chronic problems. In Lee Sechrest, Susan O. White, & Elizabeth D. Brown, *The Rehabilitation of Criminal Offenders: Problems and Prospects.* Washington, DC: National Academy of Sciences. Pp. 163–209.

Richardson, Deborah, & Jennifer L. Campbell. 1982. Alcohol and rape: The effect of alcohol on attributions of blame for rape. *Personality & Social Psychology Bulletin*, 8, 468–476.

Rimland, Bernard. 1966. Psychiatry overextended. *Science*, 154, 1395.

Risin, Leslie I., & J. Regis McNamara. 1989. Validation of child sexual abuse: The psychologist's role. *Journal of Clinical Psychology*, 45, 175–184.

Roberts, Leigh M., & Asher R. Pacht. 1965. Termination of inpatient treatment for sex deviates: Psychiatric, social, and legal factors. *American Journal of Psychiatry*, 121, 873–880.

Rodell, Fred. 1965. Our unlovable sex laws. *TransAction*, 2, 36–39.

Rodenhauser, Paul. 1984. Treatment refusal in a forensic hospital: Ill use of the lasting right. *Bulletin of the American Academy of Psychiatry & the Law*, 12, 59–63.

Rodkin, Lawrence I., E. Joan Hunt, & Suzi D. Cowan. 1982. A men's support group for "significant others" of rape victims. *Journal of Marital & Family Therapy*, 8, 91–97.

Rogers, Richard. 1986. *Conducting Insanity Evaluations.* New York: Van Nostrand Reinhold.

Rogers, Richard, & Richard Zimbarg. 1987. Antisocial backgrounds of defendants evaluated for insanity: A research note. *International Journal of Law & Psychiatry,* 10, 75–80.

Rogers, Richard, William Seman, & Orest E. Wasyliw. 1983. The RCRAS and legal insanity: A cross-validation study. *Journal of Clinical Psychology,* 39, 554–559.

Rogers, Richard, James L. Cavanaugh, William Seman, & Michael Harris. 1984. Legal outcome and clinical findings: A study of insanity evaluations. *Bulletin of the American Academy of Psychiatry & the Law,* 12, 75–83.

Roland, Billy C., Paul F. Zelhart, & Samuel W. Cochran. 1985. MMPI correlates of clinical women who report early sexual *abuse. Journal of Clinical Psychology,* 41, 763–766.

Romero, Joseph J., & Linda Meyer Williams. 1985. Recidivism among convicted sex offenders: A 10-year follow up study. *Federal Probation,* 49, 58–64.

Rose, D., & E.J. Bitter. 1982. The Palo Alto destructive content scale as a predictor of physical assaultiveness in men. *Journal of Personality Assessment,* 44, 228–233.

Rose, Vicki M., & Susan C. Randall. 1982. The impact of investigator perceptions of victim legitimacy on the processing of rape/sexual assault cases. *Symbolic Interaction,* 5, 23–36.

Rousseau, L., A. Dupont, F. LaBrie, & M. Couture. 1988. Sexuality changes in prostate cancer patients receiving antihormonal therapy combining the anti-androgren flutamide with medical (LHRH agonist) or surgical castration. *Archives of Sexual Behavior,* 17, 87–98.

Royal College of Psychiatrists. 1976. *Evidence to the Criminal Law Revision Committee on Sexual Offences.* London: The College.

Rubin, B. 1972. Prediction of dangerousness in mentally ill criminals. *Archives of General Psychiatry,* 25, 397–407.

Rubin, H.B., & Donald L. Henson. 1976. Effects of alcohol on male sexual responding. *Psychopharmacology,* 47, 123–134.

Ruch, Libby O., & Michael Hennessy. 1982. Sexual assault: Victim and attack dimensions. *Victimology,* 7, 94–105.

Ruch, Libby O., & Joseph J. Leon. 1983. Type of sexual assault trauma: A multidimensional analysis. *Victimology,* 8, 237–250.

Russell, Diana E. 1982. The prevalence and incidence of forcible rape and attempted rape of females. *Victimology,* 7, 81–93.

Sadoff, Robert L. 1975. Treatment of violent sex offenders. *International Journal of Offender Therapy & Comparative Criminology,* 19, 75–80.

Sagatun, Inger J. 1982. Attributional effects of therapy with incestuous families. *Journal of Marital & Family Therapy,* 8, 99–104.

Santiago, Jose M., Fred McCall-Perez, Michele Gorcey, & Allan Beigel. 1985. Long-term psychological effects of rape in 35 victims. *American Journal of Psychiatry,* 142, 1338–1340.

Sattem, Linda, Jerry Savelis, & Ellen Murray. 1984. Sex role stereotypes and commitment of rape. *Sex Roles,* 11, 849–860.

Schatzberg, Alan F., & Jonathan O. Cole. 1986. *Manual of Clinical Psychopharmacology.* Washington, DC: American Psychiatric Press.

Scheppele, Kim L., & Pauline B. Bart. 1983. Through women's eyes: Defining danger in the wake of sexual assault. *Journal of Social Issues,* 39, 63–80.

Schmitt, Barton D., Jane Gray, Claudia Carroll, et al. 1980. Incest and other family related sexual abuse cases: Physicians' guidelines to management. In Barbara M. Jones, Linda L. Jenstrom, & Kee MacFarlane (eds.), *Sexual Abuse of Children.* Washington, DC: National Center on Child Abuse & Neglect, U.S. Department of Health & Human Services. Pp. 135–156.

Schoenthaler, Stephen J. 1983. The Los Angeles probation department diet-behavior program: An empirical analysis of six institutional settings. *International Journal of Biosocial Research*, 5, 88–98.

Scott, Ronald L. 1982. Analysis of the need systems of twenty male rapists. *Psychological Reports*, 51, 1119–1125.

Scott, Ronald L., & David A. Stone. 1986. MMPI profile constellations in incest families. *Journal of Consulting & Clinical Psychology*, 54, 364–368.

Scott, Ronald L., & Gail Thoner. 1986. Ego deficits in anorexia nervosa patients and incest victims: An MMPI comparative analysis. *Psychological Reports*, 58, 839–546.

Scott, Ronald L., & Laurie A. Tetreault. 1987. Attitudes of rapists and other violent offenders toward women. *Journal of Social Psychology*, 127, 375–380.

Scully, Diana. 1988. Convicted rapists' perceptions of self and victim: Role taking and emotions. *Gender & Society*, 2, 200–213.

Scully, Diana, & Joseph Marolla. 1984. Convicted rapists' vocabulary of motive: Excuses and justification. *Social Problems*, 31, 530–544.

Scully, Diana, & Joseph Marolla. 1985. "Riding the bull at Gilley's": Convicted rapists describe the rewards of rape. *Social Problems*, 32, 251–263.

Sealy, A.P., & C.M. Wain. 1980. Person perception and juror's decisions. *British Journal of Social & Clinical Psychology*, 19, 7–16.

Segal, Zindel V., & William L. Marshall. 1985. Heterosexual social skills in a population of rapists and child molesters. *Journal of Consulting & Clinical Psychology*, 53, 55–63.

Seghorn, Theoharis K., Robert A. Prentky, & Richard J. Boucher. 1987. Childhood sexual abuse in the lives of sexually aggressive offenders. *Journal of the American Academy of Child & Adolescent Psychiatry*, 26, 262–267.

Serber, Michael. 1970. Shame aversion therapy. *Journal of Behaviour Therapy & Experimental Psychiatry*, 1, 213–215.

Shaalan, Mohammed, Ahmed S. El-Akaboui, & Sayed El-Kott. 1983. Rape victims in Egypt. *Victimology*, 8, 277–290.

Shannon, Lyle W. 1985. Risk assessment vs. real prediction: The prediction problem and public trust. *Journal of Quantitative Criminology*, 1, 159–189.

Shapiro, David L. 1984. Criminal responsibility: The historical background. In David L. Shapiro, *Psychological Evaluation and Expert Testimony.* New York: Van Nostrand Reinhold. Pp. 28–50.

Sharma, Anu, & Harold E. Cheatham. 1986. A women's center support group for sexual assault victims. *Journal of Counseling & Development*, 64, 525–527.

Sherlock, Richard. 1984. Compliance and responsibility: New issues for the insanity defense. *Journal of Psychiatry & Law*, 12, 483–505.

Shore, David A. 1982. Sexual abuse and sexual education in child-caring institutions. *Journal of Social Work & Human Sexuality*, 1, 171–184.

Shorts, Ivor D. 1985. Treatment of a sex offender in a maximum security forensic hospital: Detecting changes in personality and interpersonal construing. *International Journal of Offender Therapy & Comparative Criminology*, 29, 237–250.

Sigler, Robert T., & Donna Haygood. 1987. The criminalization of forced marital intercourse. *Marriage & Family Review*, 12, 71–85.

Silver, Steven W. 1976. Outpatient treatment for sexual offenders. *Social Work*, 21, 134–140.

Silver, Stuart B., & Michael K. Spodak. 1983. Dissection of the prongs of ALI: A retrospective assessment of criminal responsibility. *Bulletin of the American Academy of Psychiatry & the Law*, 11, 383–391.

Silverman, Daniel C., S. Michael Kalick, Sally I. Bowie, & Susan D. Edbril. 1988. Blitz rape and confidence rape: A typology applied to 1,000 consecutive cases. *American Journal of Psychiatry*, 145, 1438–1441.

Simon, Robert 1.1987. *Clinical Psychiatry and the Law*. Washington, DC: American Psychiatric Press.

Sinclair, Ken, & Michael W. Ross. 1985. Consequences of decriminalization of homosexuality: A study of two Australian states. *Journal of Homosexuality*, 12, 119–127.

Skodol, A.E., & T. B. Karasu. 1978. Emergency psychiatry and the assaultive patient. *American Journal of Psychiatry*, 135, 202–205.

Slicner, Nancy A., & Steven R. Hanson. 1989. Guidelines for videotape interviews in child sexual abuse cases. *American Journal of Forensic Psychology*, 7, 61–74.

Slobogin, Christopher, Gary B. Melton, & C. Robert Showalter. 1984. The feasibility of a brief evaluation of mental state at the time of the offense. *Law & Human Behavior*, 8, 305–320.

Slovenko, Ralph. 1965. *Sexual Behavior and the Law*. Springfield, IL: Charles C. Thomas.

Smeaton, George, & Donn Byrne. 1987. The effects of R-rated violence and erotica, individual differences, and victim characteristics on acquaintance rape proclivity. *Journal of Research in Personality*, 21, 171–184.

Smith, Charles E. 1968. Correctional treatment of the sexual deviate. *American Journal of Psychiatry*, 125, 615–621.

Smith, Robert J., Karen Tritt, & Andreas Zollman. 1982. Sex differences in the social perception of rape victims in West Germany and the United States. *Journal of Social Psychology*, 117, 143–144.

Smith, Roger. 1980. Scientific thought and the boundary of insanity and criminal responsibility. *Psychological Medicine*, 10, 15–23.

Smith, Wayne R., & Caren Monastersky. 1986. Assessing juvenile sexual offenders' risk for re-offending. *Criminal Justice & Behavior*, 13, 115–140.

Smith, Wayne R., Caren Monastersky, & Robert M. Deisher. 1987. MMPI-based personality types among juvenile sexual offenders. *Journal of Clinical Psychology*, 43, 422–430.

Sommers, Evelyn K., & James V. Check. 1987. An empirical investigation of the role of pornography in the verbal and physical abuse of women. *Violence & Victims*, 2, 189–209.

Steadman, Henry J., & J.J. Cocozza. 1978. Psychiatry, dangerousness, and the repetitively violent offender. *Journal of Criminal Law and Criminology*, 69, 226–231.

Steadman, Henry J., Lydia Keitner, Jeraldine Braff, & Thomas M. Arvanites. 1983. Factors associated with a successful insanity plea. *American Journal of Psychiatry*, 140, 401–405.

Steadman, Henry J., Marilyn J. Rosenstein, Robin L. MacAskill, & Ronald W. Manderscheid. 1988. A profile of mentally disordered offenders admitted to inpatient psychiatric services in the United States. *Law & Human Behavior*, 12, 91–99.

Sterling, Joanne W. 1976. An alternative model for the treatment of sex offenders. *Offender Rehabilitation*, 1, 83–87.

Stermac, Lana E., & Vernon L. Quinsey. 1986. Social competence among rapists. *Behavioral Assessment*, 8, 171–185.

Stickney, Stonewall B. 1976. *Wyatt v. Stickney:* Background and post-mortem. In Stuart Golann and William J. Fremouw (eds.), *The Right to Treatment for Mental Patients.* New York: Irvington. Pp. 29–46.

Stone, Alan A. 1976. *Mental Health and Law: A System in Transition.* New York: Jason Aronson.

Stone, Alan A. 1984. *Law, Psychiatry, and Morality.* Washington, DC: American Psychiatric Press.

Stoudemire, G. Alan. 1987. Selected organic mental disorders. In Robert E. Hales & Stuart C. Yudofsky (eds.), *American Psychiatric Press Textbook of Neuropsychiatry.* Washington, DC: American Psychiatric Press. Pp. 125–140.

Stretch, Robert H., James D. Vail, & Joseph P. Maloney. 1985. Post-traumatic stress disorder among Army Nurse Corps Vietnam veterans. *Journal of Consulting & Clinical Psychology*, 53, 704–708.

Sturup, G. 1972. Castration: The total treatment. In H.L.P. Resnick & M.W. Wolfgang (eds.), *Sexual Behaviors: Social, Clinical, and Legal Aspects.* Boston: Little, Brown. Pp. 361–382.

Summers, Montague. 1928. *The Malleus Maleficarium of Heinrich Kramer and James Sprenger.* London: John Rodker.

Swan, Helen, Allan H. Press, & Steven L. Briggs. 1985. Child sexual abuse prevention: Does it work? *Child Welfare*, 64, 395–405.

Swett, Chester, & Stuart C. Hartz. 1984. Antecedents of violent acts in a prison hospital. *American Journal of Social Psychiatry*, 4, 24–29.

Szasz, Thomas. 1987. *Insanity: The Idea and Its Consequences.* New York: Wiley.

Taylor, Michael Alan, Frederick S. Sierles, & Richard Abrams. 1987. The neuropsychiatric evaluation. In Robert E. Hales & Stuart C. Yudofsky (eds.), *The American Psychiatric Press Textbook of Neuropsychiatry.* Washington, DC: American Psychiatric Press. Pp. 3–16.

Thornton, Billy, & Richard M. Ryckman. 1983. The influence of a rape victim's attractiveness on observers' attributions of responsibility. *Human Relations*, 36, 549–561.

Thornton, Billy, Richard M. Ryckman, & Michael A. Robbins. 1982. The relationship of observer characteristics to beliefs in the causal responsibility of victims of sexual assault. *Human Relations*, 35, 321–331.

Thornton, Carolyn I., & James H. Carter. 1986. Treatment considerations with Black incestuous families. *Journal of the National Medical Association*, 78, 49–53.

Tingle, David, George W. Barnard, Lynn Robbins, & Gustave Newman. 1986. Childhood and adolescent characteristics of pedophiles and rapists. *International Journal of Law & Psychiatry*, 9, 103–116.

Tollison, C. David, & Henry E. Adams. 1979. *Sexual Disorders: Treatment, Theory, and Research.* New York: Gardner.

Tong, Liz, Kim Oates, & Michael McDowell. 1987. Personality development following sexual abuse. *Child Abuse & Neglect*, 11, 371–383.

Torrey, E. Fuller. 1988. *Nowhere to Go: The Tragic Odyssey of the Homeless Mentally Ill.* New York: Harper & Row.

Traver, Harold. 1978. Offender reaction, professional opinion, and sentencing. *Criminology*, 16, 403–419.

Truesdell, Donna L., John S. McNeil, & Jeanne P. Deschner. 1986. Incidence of wife abuse in incestuous families. *Social Work*, 31, 138–140.

Tyler, Ann H., & Marla R. Brassard. 1984. Abuse in the investigation and treatment of intrafamilial child sexual abuse. *Child Abuse & Neglect*, 8, 47–53.

Underwood, Maureen M., & Nancy Fiedler. 1983. The crisis of rape: A community response. *Community Mental Health Journal*, 19, 227–230.

Valdiserri, Edwin V., & Jessica P. Byrne. 1982. Hypnosis as emergency treatment for a teen-age rape victim. *Hospital & Community Psychiatry*, 33, 767–769.

Van Buskirk, Susan S., & Carolyn F. Cole. 1983. Characteristics of eight women seeking therapy for effects of incest. *Psychotherapy*, 20, 503–514.

Vander Mey, Brenda J., & Ronald L. Neff. 1984. Adult-child incest: A sample of substantiated cases. *Family Relations*, 33, 549–557.

Van Ness, Shela R. 1984. Rape as instrumental violence: A study of youth offenders. *Journal of Offender Counseling, Services & Rehabilitation*, 9, 161–170.

Varley, Christopher K. 1984. Schizophreniform psychoses in mentally retarded adolescent girls following sexual assault. *American Journal of Psychiatry*, 141, 593–595.

Veneziano, Carol A. 1986. Prison inmates and consent to treatment: Problems and issues. *Law & Psychology Review*, 10, 129–146.

Verleur, Donald, Ronald E. Hughes, & Marlene D. DeRios. 1986. Enhancement of self-esteem among adolescent incest victims: A controlled comparison. *Adolescence*, 21, 843–854.

Vernon, Lois J., & Connie L. Best. 1983. Assessment and treatment of rape-induced fear and anxiety. *Clinical Psychologist*, 36, 99–101.

Vinogradov, Sophia, Norman I. Dishotsky, Ann K. Doty, & Jared R. Tinklenberg. 1988. Patterns of behavior in adolescent rape. *American Journal of Orthopsychiatry*, 58, 179–187.

Virkkunen, Matti. 1982. Evidence for abnormal glucose tolerance test among violent offenders. *Neuropsychobiology*, 8, 30–34.

Virkkunen, Matti. 1983. Serum cholesterol levels in homicidal offenders: A low cholesterol level is connected with a habitually violent tendency under the influence of alcohol. *Neuropsychobiology*, 10, 65–69.

Virkkunen, Matti. 1985. Urinary free cortisol secretion in habitually violent offenders. *Acta Psychiatrica Scandinavica*, 72, 40–44.

Virkkunen, Matti. 1986. Insulin secretion during the glucose tolerance test among habitually violent and impulsive offenders. *Aggressive Behavior*, 12, 303–310.

Virkkunen, Matti, Arto Nuutila, Frederick K. Goodwin, & Markku Linnoila. 1987. Cerebrospinal fluid monamine metabolite levels in male arsonists. *Archives of General Psychiatry*, 44, 241–247.

Volcher, R. 1965. Quelques aspects medicopsychologiques de la delinquance sexuelle. *Revue de Droit Penal et de Criminologie*, 45, 837–868.

Vuocolo, Alfred B. 1968. *The Repetitive Sex Offender*. Menlo Park: New Jersey State Diagnostic Center.

Wakefield, Hollida, & Ralph Underwager. 1989. Evaluating the child witness in sexual abuse cases: Interview or inquisition? *American Journal of Forensic Psychology*, 7, 43–69.

Walker, Lenore E., & Angela Browne 1985. Gender and victimization by intimates. *Journal of Personality*, 53, 175–195.

Walsh, Anthony. 1984. Differential sentencing patterns among felony sex offenders and non-sex offenders. *Journal of Criminal Law & Criminology*, 75, 443–458.

Walsh, Anthony. 1986. Placebo justice: Victim recommendations and offender sentences in sexual assault cases. *Journal of Criminal Law & Criminology*, 77, 1126–1141.

Webster, S. 1980. Psychophysiological assessment of sex offenders in a security hospital. *Archives of Sexual Behavior*, 9, 205–216.

Weiner, Barbara A. 1985. Legal issues raised in treating sex offenders. *Behavioral Sciences & the Law*, 3, 325–340.

Weingourt, Rita. 1985. Wife rape: Barriers to identification and treatment. *American Journal of Psychotherapy*, 39, 187–192.

Weiss, Edward H. 1983. Incest accusation: Assessing credibility. *Journal of Psychiatry & Law*, 11, 305–317.

Weiss, Edward H., & R.F. Berg. 1982. Child victims of sexual assault: Impact of court procedures. *Journal of the American Academy of Child Psychiatry*, 21, 513–518.

Wenk, E.A., J.O. Robison, & G.W. Smith. 1972. Can violence be predicted? *Crime and Delinquency*, 1972, 18, 393–402.

West, Donald J., & Alexander Walk, eds. 1977. *Daniel McNaughton: His Trial and the Aftermath.* Ashford, Kent: Royal College of Psychiatrists.

Wettstein, Robert M. 1986. No Miranda warnings for alleged sexually dangerous persons. *Mental & Physical Disability Law Reporter*, 10, 326, 330.

Wettstein, Robert M. 1987. Legal aspects of neuropsychiatry. In Robert E. Hales and Stuart C. Yudofsky (eds.), *The American Psychiatric Press Textbook of Neuropsychiatry*. Washington, DC: American Psychiatric Press. Pp. 451–463.

Whitman, Steven. 1984. Epilepsy in prison: Elevated prevalence and no relationship to violence. *Neurology*, 34, 775–782.

Williams, Joyce E., & Karen A. Holmes. 1982. In judgment of victims: The social context of rape. *Journal of Sociology & Social Welfare*, 9, 154–169.

Williams, Linda S. 1984. The classic rape: When do victims report? *Social Problems*, 31, 459–467.

Williams, W., & K.S. Miller. 1977. The role of personal characteristics in perceptions of dangerousness. *Criminal Justice & Behavior*, 4, 241–252.

Wilson, G. Terence. 1977. Alcohol and human sexual behavior. *Behaviour Research & Therapy*, 15, 239–252.

Wilson, G. Terence, & David M. Lawson. 1976. Expectancies, alcohol, and sexual arousal in male social drinkers. *Journal of Abnormal Psychology*, 85, 587–594.

Wilson, G. Terence, & R. Niaura. 1984. Alcohol and the disinhibition of sexual responsiveness. *Journal of Studies on Alcohol*, 45, 219–224.

Wilson, James Q., & Richard J. Herrnstein. 1985. *Crime & Human Nature: The Definitive Study of the Causes of Crime.* New York: Simon & Schuster.

Wincze, John P., Bansal Sudhir, & Mark Malamud. 1986. Effects of medroxyprogesterone acetate on subjective arousal, arousal to erotic stimulation, and nocturnal penile tumescence in male sex offenders. *Archives of Sexual Behavior*, 15, 293–305.

Wirtz, Philip W., & Adele V. Harrell. 1987. Effects of post-assault exposure to attack-similar stimuli on long-term recovery of victims. *Journal of Consulting & Clinical Psychology*, 55, 10–16.

Wolert, Richard W., Nancy Barron, & "Bob M." 1982. Parents United of Oregon: A natural history of a self-help group for sexually abusive families. *Prevention in Human Services*, 1, 99–109.

Wolfe, Roger W., & Dominic R. Marino. 1975. A program of behavior treatment for incarcerated pedophiles. *American Criminal Law Review*, 13, 69–83.

Wood, Rodger Llewellyn. 1987. *Brain Injury Rehabilitation: A Neurobehavioral Approach.* Rockville, MD: Aspen.

Woody, Robert H. 1973. Integrated aversion therapy and psychotherapy: Two sexual deviation case studies. *Journal of Sex Research,* 9, 313–324.

World Health Organization. 1989. *International Classification of Diseases, Ninth Revision, Clinical Modification, Third Edition, Volume 1.* Washington, DC: Health Care Financing Administration, Public Health Service, U.S. Department of Health & Human Services.

Wormith, J. Stephen. 1986. Assessing deviant sexual arousal: Physiological and cognitive aspects. *Advances in Behaviour Research & Therapy,* 8, 101–137.

Wydra, Alina, W.L. Marshall, C.M. Earls, & H.E Barbaree. 1983. Identification of cues and control of sexual arousal by rapists. *Behaviour Research & Therapy,* 21, 469–476.

Wyer, Robert S., Galen V. Bodenhausen, & Theresa F. Gorman. 1985. Cognitive mediators of reactions to rape. *Journal of Personality & Social Psychology,* 48, 324–338.

Wysocki, Aydin C., & Wysocki, Boleslaw A. 1977. Human figure drawings of sex offenders. *Journal of Clinical Psychology,* 33, 278–284.

Yarmey, A. Daniel. 1985. Older and younger adults' attributions of responsibility toward rape victims and rapists. *Canadian Journal of Behavioural Science,* 17, 327–338.

Yassen, Janet, & Lois Glass. 1984. Sexual assault survivors groups: A feminist practice perspective. *Social Work,* 29, 252–257.

Yates, Alayne, Larry E. Beutler, & Marjorie Crago. 1985. Drawings by child victims of incest. *Child Abuse & Neglect,* 9, 183–189.

Yesavage, Jerome A. 1983. Correlates of dangerous inpatient behaviour. *British Journal of Psychiatry,* 143, 554–557.

Yeudall, L.T., & D. Fromm-Auch. 1979. Neuropsychological impairments in various psychopathological populations. In John Gruzelier & Pierre Flor-Henry (eds.), *Hemisphere Asymmetries of Function in Psychopathology.* Amsterdam: Elsevier/ North Holland Biomedical Press. Pp. 401–428.

Zilberg, Nathan J., Daniel S. Weiss, & Mardi J. Horowitz. 1982. Impact of event scale: A cross-validation study and some empirical evidence supporting a conceptual model of stress response syndromes. *Journal of Consulting & Clinical Psychology,* 50, 407–414.

Zimring, Franklin E., & Gordon Hawkins. 1986. *Capital Punishment and the American Agenda.* Cambridge: Cambridge University Press.

Index

For Product Safety Concerns and Information please contact our EU
representative GPSR@taylorandfrancis.com
Taylor & Francis Verlag GmbH, Kaufingerstraße 24, 80331 München, Germany